GOD'S WORD WORKS!

How You Can *Overcome* Life's
Challenges with Courage and Peace

RUTH GONZALEZ-BREWER

© Copyright 2021 by **Ruth Gonzalez-Brewer**
God's Word Works!

ISBN: 978-1-7369792-0-4 (Paperback)
ISBN: 978-1-7369792-1-1 (Ebook)

All rights reserved. No part of this publication may be reproduced, distributed or transmitted in any form or by any means, including photocopying, recording, or other electronic or mechanical methods, without the prior written permission of the publisher, except in the case of brief quotations embodied in critical reviews and certain other noncommercial uses permitted by copyright law.

Although the author and publisher have made every effort to ensure that the information in this book was correct at press time, the author and publisher do not assume and hereby disclaim any liability to any party for any loss, damage, or disruption caused by errors or omissions, whether such errors or omissions result from negligence, accident, or any other cause.

Adherence to all applicable laws and regulations, including international, federal, state and local governing professional licensing, business practices, advertising, and all other aspects of doing business in the US, Canada or any other jurisdiction is the sole responsibility of the reader and consumer.

Neither the author nor the publisher assumes any responsibility or liability whatsoever on behalf of the consumer or reader of this material. Any perceived slight of any individual or organization is purely unintentional.

Unless otherwise noted, Scripture quotations marked AMP, are taken from the Amplified ® Bible, Copyright © 1954,1958,1962, 1964, 1965, 1987 by The Lockman Foundation. Used by permission. www.Lockman.org

Unless otherwise noted, Scripture quotations marked NIV, are taken from the Holy Bible, New International Version ® , NIV ® Copyright © 1973, 1978, 1984, 2011 by Biblica, Inc.™ Used by permission. All rights reserved worldwide.

Unless otherwise noted, Scripture quotations marked KJV are taken from the King James Version of the Bible.

For more information:

www.Gods-Word-Works.com
GodsWordWorks2020@gmail.com

Free Action Guide

To get the best experience with this book, download this free Action Guide PDF for your personal study. It's meant to be used in conjunction with the book *God's Word Works! How You can Overcome Life's Challenges with Courage and Peace!*

You'll be able to implement the lessons faster as you learn God's promises and answer the questions to be able to apply them to your daily life.

Request your copy of this Free ACTION GUIDE at:

www.Gods-Word-Works.com

Dedication

To my precious children:

Melisa, Elena, Selina, Cristina, and Tony

~ I am extremely proud, and thankful to God

for each of you! I love you with all my heart! ~

Table of Contents

Free: God's Word Works ACTION GUIDE iii

Introduction 1
    Action - Introduction to God's Word Works 7

Chapter 1: The Most Devastating News of My Life 9
    Action 1—Applying God's Words 26

Chapter 2: Receiving God's Free Gift 27
    Action 2—Applying God's Words 30

Chapter 3: Overcoming Fear With Faith 31
    Action 3—Applying God's Word 35

Chapter 4: Hungry for God's Word 37
    Action 4 - Applying God's Word 41

Chapter 5: Shining for God 43
    Action 5 - Applying God's Word 47

Chapter 6: Living for God in Everyday Life 49
    Making a Difference With My Family 49
    Making a Difference in My Community 53
    Making a Difference With Women 54
    Making a Difference With the Students 57
    Action 6: Applying God's Word 64

Chapter 7: Divine Promotions 65
    Action 7: Applying God's Word 70

Chapter 8: A New Beginning 71
    Action 8: Applying God's Word 78

Chapter 9: Defeating Unexpected Challenges 79
    Action 9: Applying God's Word 86

Chapter 10: Transforming Your Life 87
    Action 10: Applying God's Word 93

Chapter 11: Putting My Love Life in God's Hands 95
    Action 11: Applying God's Word 103

Chapter 12: Handling Unexpected Disappointments 105
    Action 12: Applying God's Word 110

Chapter 13: Finding My Purpose 111
    Action 13: Applying God's Word 118

Chapter 14: Divine Connections 119
    Action 14: Applying God's Word 128

Chapter 15: The Miracle of the Transformation 129
    Action 15: Applying God's Word 138

Acknowledgements 139

Poem: "Blue Moon Blessing" 142

Have you Received God's Free Gift of Salvation? 144

Prayer for Salvation 145

Index: Promises from God's Word 147

Resources 159

Special Request 161

About the Author 162

Introduction

In late August 2012, I was faced with shocking news that would change my life forever. I was told that I had a large brain tumor, which was 4.2cm, the size of a golf ball, and it was taking over my brain. I would need brain surgery immediately. Within a week, on September 6, 2012, I underwent an eight hour brain surgery to remove my tumor, a benign Acoustic Neuroma, at the Mayo Clinic in Jacksonville, Florida. I will never stop thanking God for the miracle of still being alive and for His healing! I was facing death, but that's when I really started to live!

During that unimaginable, tragic, and desperate time, I realized that God had prepared me "for such a time as this." God's Word surfaced in my mind to empower me to positively confess and believe His Word as I was facing the fearfully unknown, and maybe even death. I believe that trusting in and confessing God's promises, which I had been learning throughout my life, helped me to go through facing this life-changing news as well as the surgery and recovery.

Throughout my life, I had been very involved in church, making a positive difference in the community, and had been studying God's Word for over 35 years. But never in my wildest imagination did I ever think that I would be facing such a terrifying and unpredictable situation. I also believe that part of my healing process was affected by an unbelievable positive attitude and strength that could only have come from God and His Word!

In my life, I had dealt with many difficulties, disappointments, and challenges. Starting with being sexually molested when I was a young girl, moving from Puerto Rico to Indiana when I was starting high school, getting married when I was 19, and being a wife and mother of five children. At that time I was also completing a Bachelor's and Master's Degree, and working as an elementary school teacher. Then after being married for 20 years, my marriage ended in divorce, I moved to Florida, changed my career, and thankfully am happily married again and enjoying health and God's blessings.

We are living in a time in which people, and including Christians, are surrounded by worry, anxiety, panic, depression, frustrations, thoughts of suicide, and even the fear of death. People are also losing their jobs, businesses, belongings, and their homes. Loved ones are getting diseases, terminal illnesses, and even dying prematurely. We're also seeing so much tragedy, hunger, floods, fires, deaths, and disasters in our world today!

Are any of these situations causing you stress and confusion and affecting your life? Where can we turn to find comfort, encouragement, hope, and promises that can help us through the challenges in this life? I believe that God and His Word, the Bible, gives us solid guidance and wisdom, as well as provide an anchor during the storms of life that we sometimes endure.

The Bible is the most read book in the world with over 3.9 billion copies printed and sold globally in the last five decades. It is one of the oldest books in the world. The full Bible has been translated into over 700 languages. What's so special about this book? Have you ever wondered who God is? What the Bible says, and does His Word work? There are many places where you can find answers. The key is that we must have faith to believe it. It's like electricity, the Internet, or the miracle of birth … we might not understand all the details about how they work, but we believe that they work and enjoy all the benefits.

I believe the Bible is our main manual for how to get to know God and His plans and purpose for our life. One of the key verses that explains how it came together is *2 Timothy 3:16–17 NIV*, *"All scripture is God-breathed and is useful for teaching, rebuking, correcting and training in righteousness, so that the servant of God may be thoroughly equipped for every good work."*

Furthermore, *Hebrews 4:12* explains how powerful it is: *"For the Word of God is alive and active. Sharper than any double-edged sword, it penetrates even to dividing soul and spirit, joints and marrow; it judges the thoughts and attitudes of the heart."* As we learn it, believe it, and apply it in our life, we are going to receive everything that God, the creator of the heavens and the earth, has promised us!

In this book, I want to share with you how I believe you can really start *living* and not just *existing* by believing the powerful promises in God's Word. For example, in *John 10:10 KJV* Jesus said, "*The thief cometh not, but for to steal, and to kill, and to destroy. I am come that they might have life, and that they might have it more abundantly.*"

If Jesus really said that, then we should expect that there must be keys and principles in God's Word that we can learn to apply to our daily life to be able to live a more abundant life. Promises about how you can have more peace, joy, courage, and confidence in your life. God has the master plan for our lives and has ultimately promised eternal life! However, I have come to realize that what we *think about, believe,* and *say* makes a difference on how any situation will affect us.

I'll also be recounting situations in which I was experiencing challenges throughout my life. After the brain surgery experience, I realized that all along God had been working in my life while I was living in Puerto Rico, Indiana, and now Florida.

After about two years after the healing of my brain surgery, on July 26, 2014, as I was sitting outside studying a morning devotional, I came across *1 Chronicles 16:8-12**. I felt that God was speaking directly to me through His Word.

> God's Word: "*Give thanks to the Lord, call on His name; make known His doings among the peoples! Sing to Him, sing praises to Him, meditate on, and talk of all His wondrous works, and devoutly praise them!*
>
> *Glory in His holy name, let the hearts of those rejoice, who seek the Lord!*
>
> *Seek the Lord, and His strength; yearn for, and seek His face and to be in His presence continually!*
>
> *(Earnestly) remember the marvelous deeds which He has done, His miracles, and the judgements He uttered (as in Egypt)*"
> - 1 Chronicles 16:8–12 AMP

While reading those verses I was encouraged to write this book so that I could share about how God works in our life, and about His miracles. I felt that He wants those who love Him to rejoice, to reach their full potential and their purpose in life.

I've been thinking about writing this book for about six years but they have have been years in which God has been working in my life increasing my wisdom, experience, and courage. I believe that He strengthens us from the inside out and that His Word works in our life even if we don't see it or feel it. God is always working!

I will be sharing with you how you can renew your mind so that you can have positive changes and see God's Word working in your life too. *Romans 12:2 KJV* clearly shows what we are to do and what the result will be: *"Be not conformed to this world: but be ye transformed (metamorphoo) by the renewing of your mind, that ye may prove what is that good, and acceptable, and perfect, will of God."*

In this book, I want to demonstrate the power of transformation (metamorphosis, the process that a caterpillar goes through to become a beautiful butterfly) as we renew our mind, so that we can face any challenges or tests that might come our way with renewed strength and confidence.

The first key is to reflect on what we're thinking about. If we don't like what's happening in our lives, we need to decide whether we need to change the situation or to change our thinking. Only *you* have the power to change *your* thinking. Then your thinking will affect your attitude, words, and actions, which will eventually affect your habits, character, and ultimately your destiny ... What have *you* been thinking lately?

Since there are obviously things that happen that we can't control in life, another significant aspect we'll learn about is the importance of releasing *"your anxiety on Him, because He cares for you" (1 Peter 5:7 NIV).* That is definitely a way to be able to experience more peace in our life. That's why one of my favorite sayings is, "I'll do my best, and let God do the rest ... and rest." We might not have control about what is happening to us, but we can control our attitude and our actions. The goal here is to keep trusting God, in other words learn to "Let Go, and Let God!"

God doesn't want us to have *religion,* but a *relationship* with Him. He loves us with an unconditional and unending love! You will be encouraged and learn key principles and God's promises to help you overcome whatever is concerning you right now.

As you will see, this book is loaded with promises labeled <u>God's Word</u>, with verses that will empower you in your daily life as you learn them. To help with this process, at the end of each chapter you'll see that there is a section called *Applying God's Word.* I encourage you to write down and study the verses and then answer the personal questions in a notebook or journal. As you do, you'll be able to build your faith, overcome fear by learning to trust God more, and experience more peace, health, and joy in your life, as God speaks to your heart! (You may also download a free copy of the *"God's Word Works" Action Guide,* which contains all of the *Applying God's Word* sections from the end of each chapter in this book.)

Will you benefit from reading this book? I definitely trust that you will! My purpose for writing this book is to be able to reach three groups of people... which one are you?

1. You that believe there is a God but don't know much about Him.
2. You want to know more about God's Word and how He works.
3. You know God and have received the gift of salvation, but desire to experience more of His power and presence to overcome life's daily challenges with courage and peace!

After you read this book, I assure you that you'll have learned an abundance of God's promises from the Bible, which will empower you to experience more peace and power in your life no matter what storms you may be going through ... *No Peace, No Power; Know Peace, Know Power!* (See Index p. 147-158.)

God's Word has definitely made a huge difference in every area of my life, and His Word can also make a difference in yours too! However, you must have the faith to believe it, the courage to confess it, and the discipline to act upon it. You only have *one life* to live. I encourage you to really start living the abundant life Jesus Christ came to make available today!

By reading this book, I trust that you'll learn to overcome any fear, even the fear of death, by understanding what I endearingly call *the Exit Plan*. Ultimately, I hope that you will understand and be assured about God's free, and gracious *plan of salvation* for you and your loved ones. With the result being that you will live more peacefully and confidently, believing that one day after we die, we'll all meet together in heaven!

It all starts by accepting God's free *gift of salvation* and spiritually becoming His son or daughter. Then you can start developing a close relationship with Him and start receiving His favor and blessings, which are promised throughout His Word to those who love, trust, and obey Him.

How many promises from God's Word do you know? Obviously, the more you know, the more you can believe for and receive in your life! So get ready to learn an abundance of promises so that you can have more courage and peace, and to overcome life's everyday challenges!

Action: Introduction to God's Word Works

Applying God's Word: 2 Timothy 3:16; Hebrews 4:12; John 10:10; Romans 12:2; 1 Peter 5:7; 1 Chronicles 16:8-12

1. Why are you interested in reading this book?
2. What are you going through right now that you want God to help you with?
3. What areas in your life do you need more courage to act on?
4. What areas in your life do you need more peace about accepting?
5. Do you believe God's Word works, or would like to know more about it?

CHAPTER 1

The Most Devastating News of My Life

<u>God's Word</u>: *"Yes, though I walk through the (deep, sunless) valley of the shadow of death, I will fear or dread no evil, for You are with me; Your rod (to protect) and Your staff (to guide), they comfort me." -Psalm 23:4*

It was 2011, and I was in my 50's. I'd been healthy all my life and only took vitamins to maintain my health. Towards the end of the year, I started to notice that when I spoke on the phone I could not hear as well from my right ear, compared to my left one. I didn't think much of it, and it didn't bother me, I just used my left ear when I had to use my cell phone.

For many months, my mother, Iris, encouraged me to get a hearing aid to help me hear better. She used to give me ads she would get in the mail about "hearing screenings." I would thank her and said I'd go someday, but I ended up ignoring most of them. However, since she kept insisting that I should go get my hearing checked, I finally decided to make an appointment and went for a screening.

The first place where I went in April 2012, the audiologist completed the screening, confirmed that I had about 30% hearing loss in my right ear, and was ready to sell me a hearing aid right away. I felt a little rushed, and wasn't ready to spend the almost $2,000 on one so I told him I'd think about it and get back to him later.

A few months passed, and then in July of 2012, my mother again told me that there was going to be a hearing screening at her church on Sunday and asked me to please go. I decided to go. The doctor who did the screening confirmed there was definitely about 30% hearing loss and suggested that I should go to her office for a more comprehensive hearing test.

I made an appointment. After she examined me, instead of trying to sell me a hearing aid, like the other place had tried to do, she encouraged me to first go to an ENT doctor (an ear, nose, and throat specialist). She wanted to make sure that we ruled out that there was nothing else going on in my head.

She also mentioned that the ENT might recommend that I get a brain MRI (Magnetic Resonance Imaging) to find out if there was anything that would be causing my hearing loss, since it was only in my left ear. I still felt hesitant about going to the ENT, because I felt fine, so I procrastinated about it.

Then, at the beginning of August of 2012, I started feeling a little dizzy, so I decided I better make an appointment to go see the ENT doctor and to find out his diagnosis. He again confirmed that I had hearing loss and advised me to make an appointment to get a brain MRI. He definitely wanted to find the cause for my hearing loss.

On the morning of Tuesday, August 28, 2012, I finally headed out to get my first brain MRI ever. It was somewhat intimidating to see the cylinder that my whole body would have to be rolled into for the test. The MRI scanner made loud banging noises during the procedure, so they made me wear headgear, but it was painless. I laid there very still for about one hour, then I was dismissed and headed home to get back to my home office.

About an hour after I got home from the brain MRI appointment, I got a call from my ENT doctor's office saying that they needed to speak with me about the MRI results immediately. I was very surprised since they had previously made an appointment for me to go the next week to find out the results.

Interestingly enough, my only sister, Mimi, had just *happened* to stop by my house, because she was facing a difficult situation and needed my input. She heard me speaking on the phone, not even realizing that I had just had an MRI, and was very perplexed when I started to ask questions about needing to go to the doctor right away.

When I got off the phone, I explained that I had just had an MRI of my brain, and that the doctor needed to see me urgently. Mimi was immediately concerned and said she wanted to go to the doctor's office with me to find out what was happening and why they needed to see me right away.

Without thinking twice about it, *my issue* became the priority, and the problem she had stopped by to discuss didn't seem that important. (It was amazing how God had set this up, so that she was there with me, because of what was about to happen!)

We arrived at the doctor's office within 30 minutes. We walked in wondering what would've been the reason why they wanted to see me so urgently. We nervously waited to be called in to see the doctor. The nurse assistant walked out, thanked us for coming so promptly, and directed us to sit and wait in the exam room.

Shortly after, the doctor walked in, kindly greeted us, and proceeded to tell us there were some urgent results from the brain MRI that needed to be discussed immediately. He carefully showed us a scan where a gigantic mass (the size of a golf ball) was pushing against my brain stem. He expounded that it was an extremely dangerous brain tumor and that I would need surgery to get it removed by the end of the week!

We looked at each other speechless! To try to ease the shock, the doctor added that it was a benign tumor called an "acoustic neuroma," and that it was not a malignant tumor. However, it had to be removed or else if it kept growing it could cause my brain stem to collapse, and I would probably die.

We sat there stunned and in disbelief! It was the biggest SHOCK and most devastating news of my LIFE! I thought..."Was this really happening to me?" It didn't even seem real since I was not in pain, and my body was functioning fine.

Right away so many questions, doubts, and concerns came to my mind. What would happen? Would I die? How about my husband, my mom, my kids, and my family? My whole world had shifted, and I felt that it would never be the same. Was death knocking at my door?

We walked out of the office dumbfounded! I felt so numb and overwhelmed with the news that I didn't even know what to make of it. All I knew is that I wasn't ready for this. The first thought that came to my head was, "But wait, I'm not ready to die, I'm not done with my work for God here on earth!" I loved God and for years I felt that my purpose in life was to spread His message of salvation and the abundant life Jesus had come to make available. I felt that I still had work to do to reach more people, especially all my loved ones.

Mimi and I stood in the parking lot by my car deeply disturbed. My mind was going in so many directions. As I pondered shaking my head tears started to fill my eyes. Mimi was frantically searching for something to say. Not knowing what to say, in desperation, she looked up to heaven as she was asking God for what to say. Then she immediately grabbed me by my shoulders and shook me as she intently stared into my eyes and lovingly yelled, "Where is your FAITH?"

Her words were like a glass of cold water splashing on my face. My eyes grew wide, and I hesitated, but all of a sudden, like a mighty lightning from heaven, I gained strength and confidently asked myself, "Yes, what about my Faith?" I immediately stopped my wandering and hopeless mind, I took a deep breath and realized that GOD was right there with me!

Suddenly, I started to remember the many promises from God's Word, which I had been learning from studying His Word all my life. Instantly, as I took a deep breath, I felt an indescribable fortitude! The first promise that came to my mind was *Romans 8:28 KJV*, which says, *"And we know that all things work together for good, to them that love God, to them who are called according to his purpose!"*

I slowly repeated the promise and knew that it was for me, because I *loved God* and felt I was *called* according to *His purpose*. So instead of asking God *why* is this happening to me, I immediately asked God, *for what purpose* is this happening to me? I felt deep inside that God would be glorified through THIS and that I needed to trust Him!

While driving in the car, still in disbelief, I started reminding myself about more of God's promises out loud, and as I did, I started to feel more confident that God would help me to get through this. As I thought about God and quietly prayed, a peace that surpasses all understanding, promised in His Word, started to calm me down.

> God's Word: "*Do not be anxious about anything, but in every situation, by prayer and petition, with thanksgiving, present your requests to God. And the peace of God, which transcends all understanding, will guard your hearts and your minds in Christ Jesus.*" -Philippians 4: 6–7 NIV

I felt that peace to the extent that I thought, that even if I ended up dying, I knew where my eternal home would be. However, my urgent mission and desperation became that I wanted to tell ALL my loved ones about God's *Plan of Salvation* so that I could see them again in Heaven!

It sure wasn't going to be easy breaking the news to my family. I am so thankful that Mimi was with me. The first place we decided to go in person to share the devastating news was with my husband, Dale, at work. Then we were planning to go to our mom's apartment.

At that time, Mimi and I also started talking about the challenge of sharing the dreadful news with my five grown children and the rest of my family and friends. How should we tell them? What would they say? How would it affect them?

We shared the news the best way we could. They were all devastated at first, as if I was announcing a *death sentence*. I explained the situation and decided to follow the *horrible news* by confessing my faith with what God has promised in His Word. My desire was to sound hopeful, and to boldly share my faith in God!

I felt it was an urgent moment to share that we needed to trust and believe that God was with me and that we didn't have to panic, because God always has the *master plan*. My family knew that I had spent most of my life, over 35 years, studying and teaching God's Promises. I knew that this was *my* opportunity to *really* believe them, to be strong, and to apply all my lessons previously learned to this experience.

I also thought it would be a vital time to share with them about what I endearingly called the *Exit Plan*, by letting them know that no matter what would happen, whether I lived or died, that we could meet in heaven. My main desire and request for them was to please accept Christ as their Savior, to trust and believe in their heart that God raised Him from the dead so that they too would be saved and we could be together again in heaven. That is our true hope! (Do you know of any other?)

> <u>God's Word</u>: *"If you declare with your mouth, 'Jesus is Lord,' and believe in your heart that God raised him from the dead, you will be saved. For it is with your heart that you believe and are justified, and it is with your mouth that you profess your faith and are saved."* -Romans 10:9–10

The preparations continued regarding my work, household responsibilities, and finances. We focused on doing our best to prepare for this life changing and unpredictable major brain surgery. We also had to be ready in case I would be disabled, paralyzed, forget everything I knew, or even died.

In addition, we had to find someone to prepare a final Will and Testament. As we diligently worked on all this, we hoped and prayed for the best, but prepared for the worst.

During this incredibly difficult time, I continued to use my knowledge of God's Word to keep sad and fearful thoughts aside. God gave me a supernatural strength! I became determined not to worry, but prayed to God and stayed connected to His peace. With God's help, I felt that I was also encouraging my family by continuing to remain as positive as possible.

God is so wonderful that to continue to keep me encouraged He even gave me a *theme song* that always energized me and took me to another level! I kept hearing the song "Our God" by Chris Tomlin on the radio. Every time I heard the words, they got me fired-up about God's miracles; that *He is our healer*, that *He is awesome in power*, and that if *He is for us, no one can ever stop us*! (Most of the words are promises from Romans 8:31-39.) My family was inspired as well, and we sure smiled every time we'd hear it on the radio. Hearing it reinforced our belief that God was really with us, and it built up our faith!

Going through this experience made me realize that life is so fragile! Sometimes we focus on material things, but yet when we're facing an unexpected tragedy or even death, our priorities definitely shift. We start focusing on things we could've and should've done or said to our loved ones.

That time of my life was a wake up call for me to really start *living* life and not existing. Of becoming more *present* in my daily life, and not just going through the *motions* of life. Being more thankful, and expressing my love to others. And being more intentional about having a fulfilled and meaningful life.

During the days leading up to my brain surgery, my daughter Elena was also nine months pregnant and almost ready to give birth to her first baby. I was looking forward to that miraculous and happy event, and to be with her during this extra special time. However, the need for the upcoming surgery had also shifted my focus. I realized that I wouldn't be able to be there for the final preparations and celebration of baby Emma's arrival. I was also sad that I wouldn't be available to help Elena as a first time mother, nor to provide my support.

The weekend before the necessary brain tumor surgery was very emotional and memorable. On Friday evening, two of my daughters, Elena and Selina, had come by my home so we could go out to dinner together (Elena lived in town, but Selina had driven down from Orlando to be with me for the weekend.) Then, as we were sitting around sharing stories in my living room, all of a sudden we were startled by someone knocking on the front door. I went to answer and was shocked to see a man dressed as a beekeeper, with a full bright yellow suit and a hat with a net over his face.

He started to tell me that there was a bee problem in my neighborhood and that he was going to be inspecting the outside of my home. At that point, my daughter Elena came to the door, and not hearing what he had told me asked him, "What are you doing here?" Unexpectedly, the beekeeper took his hat off and said "I'm looking for my mother!"

He stepped inside the house and immediately reached out to hug me and told me, "I love you mom"! WOW, it was my son, Tony! I hadn't seen him in a few years, but when he heard about the upcoming brain surgery, he flew down from Indiana to surprise me. I was so shocked and super excited to see him that I began to scream and cried tears of joy! It sure was an incredible blessing to have reunited with him!

After that amazing surprise, he joined us, and we all went out to dinner. After dinner, we had made arrangements that we were going to meet my sister Mimi and her two boys, Jimmy and Mikey, at Siesta Key Beach. We wanted to go there that evening, because on that night, we were going to witness a "Blue Moon" in the sky.

A "Blue Moon" is a fairly infrequent phenomenon, when two full moons show up in a 30-day lunar cycle, so we didn't want to miss it. The moon is also usually closer to the horizon, appearing much larger to the viewer. That night it lit up the beach almost as if it was daylight ... a truly amazing sight to see!

To make it even more special, Mimi had written a beautiful and heartwarming poem about me called "Blue Moon Blessing"! She read it while we all stood with our feet in the sand, admiring the "Blue Moon." In it she mentioned how I was so kind, helped others, and was rare, like the blue moon itself. I will remember forever how her poem touched my heart, humbled me, and made me cry tears of thankfulness, and love!

> *Once in a Blue Moon we find someone like you*
> *Someone trusting and friendly so honest and true.*
> *I've written this poem from my heart and my mind*
> *To you, my dear sister, so loving and kind.*
>
> *(You may read the rest of the poem in the back of the book.)*

<u>God's Word</u>: *"The Lord watches over you -the Lord is your shade at your right hand; the sun will not harm you by day, nor the moon by night. The Lord will keep you from all harm — he will watch over your life the Lord will watch over your coming and going both now and forevermore." -Psalm 121:5–8*

Very late that evening, after we got back from Siesta Key Beach, my son Tony, my daughter Selina, and I, ended up chatting by my kitchen counter. Even though it was late, I felt energized as my heart was beating at a fast and happy pace while we were together. I started sharing about God's promises, and they were intensely and quietly listening.

In amazement, Selina stopped me and asked, "Mom, how could you be so positive, when something so tragic is happening to you?" At that moment, I stopped to think and was dumbfounded, not knowing what to answer. I quickly gathered my thoughts and said, "What other way is there to be … to run to my room, cry, and hide my head under my pillow, feeling sorry for myself, or be angry that this is happening to me?"

In that moment I suddenly realized that many of God's promises that I'd been learning throughout my life, were now spilling out of the depths of my soul, as I was sharing with my children. I thought about an example, and explained to them, "It's just like a coffee cup with no lid. When someone bumps you, or like in this situation, when life's challenges bump you, what's inside of you spills out."

> God's Word: "...*For out of the fullness (the overflow, the super abundance) of the heart the mouth speaks."*
> -Matthew 12:34b AMP

As I was sharing these things, at that moment, I felt in my spirit that all my life God had been preparing me for *"such a time as this,"* just like in *Esther 4:14*; that *this* was the moment I needed to be strong, and to trust God with all my heart!

It was awesome to feel that God was truly with me, and His power was strengthening me throughout that whole storm! However, I realized that not knowing what was to happen I would need someone to be strong for me, just in case I got weak. So as Selina and I were sitting on the couch thinking about what I was going to go through, I made an instant request, "I'm strong now, but if I get weak, would you please be strong for me?"

Not ever expecting that question, and still very concerned about the outcome, her eyes opened wide, not knowing how to respond. All of a sudden, she gained confidence and lovingly told me, "Yes Mom, I'll be strong for you!" I truly believe that going through that experience was a real life transforming wake-up call to life for her that changed her whole perspective on life.

Since then, Selina has overcome mental and physical challenges. She has been promoted at work several times, was able to transfer her job to San Francisco, CA, and is now living and working in London, England. She's really enjoying the life of her dreams and has been able to travel extensively.

For the first three years since she moved to London, she also treated me to what we like to call our "Mother-Daughter World Adventures." We've planned the trips during May to celebrate Mother's Day together. We've been to Portugal, Switzerland, and on a cruise of the Greek Isles. Unfortunately, in 2020, we were forced to cancel our trip due to Covid-19. I am truly delighted that God has blessed her abundantly!

> God's Word: *"The fear of man brings a snare, but whoever leans on, trusts in, and puts his confidence in the Lord is safe and set on high."* -Proverbs 29:25

My family and I continued trying to find the best medical help for the brain surgery. Due to the diligence, persistence, and help of my dear mother Iris and sister Mimi (and along with some "favor" from above, I believe), we were able to get an appointment right away, at the Mayo Clinic in Jacksonville, Florida, which is regarded as one of the best hospitals in the world.

As an added blessing, the doctor that we were scheduled to see ended up being the chairman of Mayo's Department of Neurosurgery! We were in absolute awe that exactly one week after the brain tumor diagnosis, Mimi, my mom, my husband Dale, and I would be taking the five hour drive up to the Mayo Clinic.

We arrived at the hospital and sat in the waiting room of the Neurosurgeon's office. My daughter Cristina also drove up from Orlando, Florida to join us. All five of us reviewed the long lists of questions we had prepared to ask the doctor as we nervously waited to meet him and to hear what he was going to say about the MRI images, about the surgery, and about possible side effects.

After waiting briefly, Dr. Wilson walked into the office and greeted us warmly, a little surprised to see all of us there. I introduced my family and explained why we were there. He asked a few questions and then requested the copy of the MRI images. He reviewed them and said that the tumor was a slow growing tumor, but it needed to be removed as soon as possible because it was pushing against my brainstem, and if it collapsed, I would instantly die. After he did a few preliminary exams on me, he was quite surprised and bewildered that I didn't have any other symptoms besides losing some of my hearing and rarely being dizzy.

We asked Dr. Wilson about the method used and any possible side effects of having this kind of surgery. He mentioned that even though some doctors use the "scooping" method, he shared that the Mayo doctors use the "draining" method to get the tumor mass out so they would avoid damaging the delicate nerves that control the face and that would cause a "droopy eye." He added that some of the possible side effects would be a hearing loss of my right ear, ringing in the affected ear, loss of balance, dizziness, and facial numbness.

As I was hearing this, one of my biggest concerns was how my memory would be affected and any other long-term side effects. As we spoke with him, we were able to confirm what we had researched, that he was very experienced, meticulous, and very passionate about his work. I was confident and wanted to hear more about the next steps.

He further explained that the surgery would take between five to eight hours. In addition, it would also have to be performed by himself and Dr. Lewis, an otolaryngologist (an ear surgeon), because the tumor had started in my right ear and expanded to the brain area. It was definitely going to be a very delicate operation.

Dr. Wilson then told us that before he could set a date for the surgery, he needed to ask Dr. Lewis. He was unsure about his schedule but felt we'd be looking at a few weeks before the surgery could be coordinated between the two surgeons' schedules. He said his staff would let us know and that we could come back up for the surgery later.

When I heard that I would probably have to wait a few weeks, I was extremely unsettled because I wanted the tumor out of my head as soon as possible. In desperation, I decided to ask him about the size of my tumor compared to others on which he had performed surgery on. He said that mine was "gigantic." At that moment, I got very emotional and said, "Is there any way we can do the surgery sooner than a few weeks?" He didn't think it would be possible, but he said that he'd be willing to check and see what could be done.

We all waited nervously, and also prayerfully. After about 20 minutes, Dr. Wilson walked in the room with a big smile, shaking his head in disbelief, and said, "Young lady, this is your lucky day. Dr. Lewis and I are both miraculously available to do your surgery tomorrow morning!" He was definitely surprised that both of them "happened" to be available to perform the surgery. We were overjoyed and thankful to God for granting us that unbelievable favor! Dr. Wilson then provided me with the presurgery orders and instructions. I was very relieved that the tumor would be removed the next day!

> God's Word: *"Let love and faithfulness never leave you; bind them around your neck and write them on the tablet of your heart. Then you will win favor and a good name in the sight of God and man." -Proverbs 3:3–4 NIV*

It was Sept. 6, 2012, my family and I got up very early and made our way to the waiting room for me to be called back into the surgery. While we sat there, and right before they were due to call me in, I told my family that I wanted to have a word of prayer with them.

We all stood in a circle, and I prayed with a thankful attitude for the doctors and nurses, as well as for peace for my family, and that the surgery would be a success. I also prayed that even if I didn't make it out alive, that we would all know that we'd see each other in heaven (our *Exit Plan*). I encouraged them to trust God, and that no matter what the outcome would end up being, that "all things would work together for good" in the mighty name of Jesus Christ! We were all in tears and hugged each other.

Shortly after the prayer, the nurse called my name. I confidently walked toward her as I waved to my family with a big smile and a thumbs up! I don't think I would've ever had that kind of confidence or felt that kind of peace if it hadn't been for my faith in God! His Word was definitely working in my life! I had no doubt that I was in God's loving arms!

> God's Word: *"Heal me, Lord, and I will be healed: save me and I will be saved, for you are the one I praise."*
> -Jeremiah 17:14

The surgery was supposed to take from five to eight hours. However, after the sixth hour, my family, who had been anxiously waiting, started to get concerned about me and why it was taking so long. They decided to ask at the information desk because they were getting worried. A phone call was made, and an actual nurse from the operating room came out to confirm that the surgery was going well and that I was ok.

They kept waiting and waiting, and *after eight long hours*, they were finally told they could go see me briefly. I opened my eyes and saw Mimi with a big smile, and I groggily said, without realizing the surgery was over, "I'll see you on the other side" (referring to when the surgery would be over), but she joyfully exclaimed, "You ARE on the other side!" I smiled and just laid there with a white bandage around my head, still under the numbness of the anesthesia. I was so relieved that the surgery was over and extremely thankful to God that I was still alive, and then I fell back asleep.

The next time I opened my eyes, I was already in my hospital room. I was so blessed to see my family there. We were all alleviated that the surgery had gone well. I could barely stand up or even walk because I was so dizzy, but I slowly gained strength.

I noticed that my vision was also affected, as everything looked blurry, even with my glasses on. Thankfully, after a few weeks my eyesight fully recovered. It was truly a blessing that I barely got headaches, and the perfectly sewn stitches behind my right ear did not hurt or bother me.

> God's Word: *"He sent His word and healed them; he rescued them from the grave."* -Psalm 107:20

While still in recovery and before I was released, it was explained to me that most of the brain tumor mass had been drained through my skull behind my right ear. However, they had left a small portion of the mass (the size of a pea) because they didn't want to affect any facial nerves. Dr. Wilson asked me to return in six months so they could perform radiation directly on the small tumor portion still left in my head. This would kill any cells that would try to grow back.

It is miraculous that after such a serious and delicate surgery, I was released to go back home after only four days following the surgery. I decided to start calling the tumor "the alien," because it doesn't belong to me, and I'm not claiming it! I've had about 10 MRIs since 2012 to monitor it and make sure it's not growing. Thank God, it has been shrinking; it's now like a scab. I believe "the alien" is destroyed now and doesn't have any power over me!

During that whole time, it was the knowledge of God's promises and the "tests" I had passed in my life that prepared me for this season. Because of God's Word, which I had planted in my heart, I was able to renew my mind and to think and confess God's promises. I truly believe that was a key element to my recovery. Even the doctors at the Mayo Clinic mentioned to me that my attitude greatly contributed to my healing process. To God be the Glory!

I unfortunately ended up losing total hearing from my right ear, but I am extremely thankful that I have a healthy left ear! When I got back home, I was off work for three months. I had to use a walker for a few weeks, as I was still experiencing a lot of dizziness while my brain was healing.

Also as I was recuperating, I was unable and not allowed to drive for three months. Mimi, took me under her wing and cared for me daily for about a month in her home and made sure I had ongoing needed assistance. She has definitely been a God-sent throughout my life!

After I went back to my home, my husband Dale was very supportive, caring, and encouraging during my rehabilitation process. Besides faithfully going to work, he always checked on me daily by calling from work and stopping by our home during the day. He also made sure all my needs were met, cooked, bought groceries, cleaned, and also washed clothes. He has always been an exceptional and loving husband!

I am also extremely thankful for the part that each of my five grown children, Melisa, Elena, Selina, Cristina, and Tony, played during that time. No matter if they were near or far, I felt they were right there with me. Calling and checking-in with me, praying, and encouraging me throughout my healing process.

Even my two grandchildren, Nick and Melodie, and Melisa's husband Pat, also called me from Indiana to send their love and to let me know that they were also praying for me!

Baby Emma, Elena and husband Rob's daughter, was actually born 10 days after the brain surgery, such a precious miracle! I was thankful that everything worked out well, even though I missed not being able to fully participate in welcoming her to the world!

I was also especially appreciative that I had my dear mom Iris there for me. At 79, she had been diagnosed with a heart problem and was told by the doctors in our city that she was supposed to have open heart surgery within a month, or she would die. However, after a second opinion at the Mayo Clinic, she decided that it was best not to have the surgery. I believe that God kept her alive for an extra 1.5 years to be around so she could be there for me during such a tragic and necessary time in my life. She was truly my *life giving* and *life saving* angel!

Because of my mom's outstanding health care and wonderful contacts at the Mayo Clinic, she wanted to make sure I went there to have the brain surgery. I truly believe that if it wasn't for her, I might not be alive today. She was the *angel* God used to pressure me to take care of my hearing loss, that ultimately resulted in the discovery of the major brain tumor, which left undetected would've caused my death.

I believe she also made a difference in us receiving God's *favor* to be able to have the surgery at the Mayo Clinic. God allowed my mom to keep living for even an extra eight months after my brain surgery, so I was also able to care for her during the last months of her life.

One of the last special memories I have of my mom is when she invited our family to celebrate Mother's Day Brunch on Sunday, May 12, 2013 in the very elegant dining room at Sarasota Bay Club where she lived. There were about 20 of our family members from near and far, and we all enjoyed a spectacular buffet of food.

An unforgettable moment was when my daughter, Melisa, took my mom and sat her in a chair in the middle of the dining hall and sang a solo accompanied by the guitar player that was there. It was an extremely beautiful expression of love. We were all touched by that occasion.

Mom's health had been very fragile, but she kept trying to be strong, was mentally sharp, and still full of determination to live. However, the very next day after our impressive Mother's Day Brunch she ended up in the hospital again. There they gave her some medicine that caused her to go into an induced coma. Unfortunately, on Friday, May 17, 2013, she went home to be with the Lord and to join my dad Nick in heaven.

My mom's death was very difficult for us, as you can imagine. She was a devoted wife, mother, grandmother, professor, and God-loving woman. She was always there for us, was an excellent role model, always loving us, and encouraging us to be the best we could be. During her funeral, because of the faith and the hope we have that we will see her again, God put in my heart to share a very special passage from the Bible in *1 Thessalonians 4:13–18* to encourage everyone at the funeral service.

> God's Word: *"Brothers and sisters, we do not want you to be uninformed about those who sleep in death, so that you do not grieve like the rest of mankind, who have no hope. For we believe that Jesus died and rose again, and so we believe that God will bring with Jesus those who have fallen asleep in him. According to the Lord's word, we tell you that we who are still alive, who are left until the coming of the Lord, will certainly not precede those who have fallen asleep. For the Lord himself will come down from heaven, with a loud command, with the voice of the archangel and with the trumpet call of God, and the dead in Christ will rise first. After that, we who are still alive and are left will be caught up together with them in*

the clouds to meet the Lord in the air. And so we will be with the Lord forever. Therefore encourage one another with these words." -1 Thessalonians 4:13–18

Having gone through my mom's death, and the experience of personally facing death was like a *wake-up call to life* for me! It made me more aware of the fact that we can't take each day or our life for granted, as we never know when our last day on earth will be.

It is such a privilege to receive the free gift of Salvation through Jesus Christ, and to have the promise of eternal life. Whether we live or die, we can rejoice in the hope that someday we will all be together forever in His presence. We don't have to be afraid of death, when we have an *Exit Plan*, which is our hope!

I have decided to continue to keep God first in my life, now more than ever, and to be more sensitive so I can hear His "still quiet voice." My passion and reason for living has become to spread His message and to make a positive difference for His kingdom here on earth.

Instead of living in the past, and with condemnation and regrets, I have made it a point to forgive others and myself, and to live in peace, as this is God's will. I have also quit trying to change my past, since I can't change it, and am focusing on the *present*, because it is a *gift* from God. I have definitely stopped just *existing* and have started *living*, taking time to "smell the roses" and finding something to be thankful for every single day!

No matter what storms we go through in life, we have to choose to trust God and not to look at our circumstances and live in fear. I hope that you've been able to see the value in having an intimate relationship with God and to trust Him, as well as seeing the value of knowing, believing, and claiming His promises!

> God's Word: *"I have told you these things, so that in Me you may have (perfect) peace and confidence. In the world you will have tribulation and trials and distress and frustration; but be of good cheer (take courage; be confident, certain, undaunted)! For I have overcome the world. (I have deprived it of power to harm you and have conquered it for you.)" -John 16:33 AMP*

Always remember, that even though we go through challenges, difficulties, or temptations in life, whether they are physical, mental, emotional, or spiritual, we *can overcome*. As we trust God and believe His promises, He will give us the courage to face our challenges and the peace to let go and let God work to fulfill His perfect plan and purpose for our life!

Everyday is a new beginning. You can choose to be pitiful or powerful, but you can't be both. It all comes down to what we think, what we say, and what we do. We need to move towards studying, believing, and acting on God's Word, which will help us trust God more, and we will fulfill His ultimate plan and purpose for us with courage and peace!

Action—Chapter 1: The Most Devastating News of My Life

Applying God's Word: Psalm 23:4; Romans 8:28; Romans 8:31–39; Philippians 4:6–7; Romans 10:9–10; Psalm 121:5–8; Matthew 12:34b; Proverbs 29:25; Proverbs 3:3–4; Jeremiah 17:14; Psalm 107:20; I Thessalonians 4:13–18; John 16:33.

1. Have you ever had any unexpected, shocking, or devastating news in your life?
2. How were you able to get through that situation in your life?
3. How has that experience changed your perspective in life?
4. Should we be afraid of death? Why or why not?
5. What is a promise in God's Word that would mentally strengthen you through difficult times?

Chapter 2

Receiving God's Free Gift

<u>God's Word:</u> *"So faith comes by hearing (what is told), and what is heard comes by the preaching (of the message that came from the lips) of Christ (the Messiah Himself)." -Romans 17:10*

Where did my interest and love for God's Word begin? I was born in San Juan, Puerto Rico to Reverend Dr. Nicandro E. Gonzalez, a Presbyterian pastor, and Dr. Iris Grace Gonzalez, a professor at the University of Puerto Rico. I grew up with two brothers, David and Daniel, and my only sister, Mimi. Since my father was a pastor, church was a major part of our activities and our life.

Things I always remember about my upbringing was that my father always loved God's Word and was committed to teaching it. He also preached very powerful messages. I recall him holding his Bible and lifting it up in the air on Sunday mornings and encouraging the people to bring others to church so they could also learn God's Word. So from a very young age, I remember that God's Word was taking root in my heart, and I was developing a hunger to understand it and to know more about why it was so special.

As I was growing up, my parents always sent us mostly to private schools in Puerto Rico so we could study and learn English, and then we would speak in Spanish at home. Spanish is the main language in the island, but most people are bilingual, since Puerto Rico is a Commonwealth of the United States. I am extremely thankful that my parents emphasized the importance of learning two languages, as it has allowed me to help people by speaking both English and Spanish.

I remember when I was in third grade our family moved to New York City for my parents to study while they were pursuing and completing their Master's degrees. We lived there only for one year, then my parents returned to Puerto Rico to continue their professions. I continued to live on the island and went to school there up to eighth grade. No matter where we lived, church was always an extra special time, and I always enjoyed learning the Bible stories.

> God's Word: *"Train up a child in the way he should go: and when he is old, he will not depart from it." -Proverbs 22:6 KJV*

When I was about 12 years old, my dad was on an area-wide committee of church leaders that were bringing Rev. Billy Graham to speak at the Hiram Bithorn Baseball Stadium in Puerto Rico. He was one of the most influential and well-known Christian preachers during that time. I remember the stadium being packed with thousands of people. From far away, I could see my father sitting on the stage with all the other pastors and leaders. I was in the stands with my family, very impressed and excited that so many people had attended to learn more about God and His Word.

I was astounded by the hundreds of people in the choir as they sang loudly and powerfully. Everyone was looking forward to the words that Rev. Graham was going to passionately speak. He shared a life transforming message from *John 3:16–17*, which says, *"For God so loved the world, that he gave his only begotten Son, that whosoever believeth in Him should not perish, but have everlasting life. For God sent not his son into the world to condemn the world; but that the world through him might be saved."*

For the first time in my life, I realized that Jesus loved me so much, that He died for me so I could have eternal life. I understood that salvation was a free gift and that all I had to do was to believe in Him. Everything Rev. Graham was saying was very meaningful to me. I remember crying about how sad it was that Jesus died on the cross *for me* to pay for all my sins. What an amazing gift of sacrifice and love!

As was his custom at the end of his messages, Rev. Graham invited people to receive Christ as their savior. I saw hundreds of hands go up. My heart started to beat fast, and I was getting very emotional. At that moment, I decided I also wanted to accept Christ's gift of salvation and decided to put my hand up. Then he asked all the people that had accepted Christ to come down to the front of the stage. I remember the enormous angelic choir singing "Just As I Am." It was so beautiful! I was humbled and very emotional to see all the hundreds of people who had just accepted Christ walking down to the front!

> God's Word: *"If you declare with your mouth, 'Jesus is Lord,' and believe in your heart that God raised him from the dead, you will be saved. For it is with your heart that you believe and are justified, and it is with your mouth that you profess your faith and are saved."* -Romans 10:9–10 NIV

I was a little intimidated as I nervously walked down and arrived at the front, not knowing what was going to happen. When I arrived by the stage, I got to see my father up close, and I was so proud and thankful for his wonderful example and leadership in being involved with such a life-changing event.

I was also very much impacted when one of the volunteers came up to speak with me. He congratulated me on my decision to accept Christ and gave me a little book, which was the Gospel of John from the Bible. I felt like I was so special and that I was really God's child! I was eager to begin my new life with Christ and to learn more about the Bible.

> God's Word: *"For it is by Grace you have been saved, through faith—and this is not from yourselves, it is the gift of God—not by works, so that no one can boast."* -Ephesians 2:8–9

Even though I was only 12, I remember how special it was to be a part of that incredible experience. To this day, I get very emotional when people humbly receive Christ as their saviour, and I think that experience is the reason why!

Salvation is a priceless free gift from God, for us to accept and receive, just by believing in Christ! At that moment, we become God's son or daughter, are spiritually *born again*, and have been promised an eternal home with God in heaven!

> God's Word: *"This is good, and pleases God our Savior, who wants all people to be saved and to come to a knowledge of the truth."* -1 Timothy 2:3-4

God's Word: *"Therefore, if anyone is in Christ, the new creation has come: The old has gone, the new is here!"*
-2 Corinthians 5:17

Action—Chapter 2: Receiving God's Free Gift

Applying God's Word: Romans 17:10; Proverbs 22:6; John 3:16–17; Romans 10:9–10; Ephesians 2:8–9; 1 Timothy 2:3-4; 2 Corinthians 5:17

1. What was your childhood like?
2. Do you remember who you looked up to and how they influenced your life?
3. Have you ever accepted Christ's invitation to be your personal savior?
4. If so, what was your experience like?
5. If not, would you like to receive Christ or know more about Him? (See p.144-145)
6. What do you need to **believe** to receive the gift of eternal life?

Chapter 3

Overcoming Fear With Faith

<u>God's Word:</u> *"Fear not (there is nothing to fear), For I am with you; do not look around you in terror and be dismayed, for I am your God. I will strengthen and harden you to difficulties, yes I will help you; yes, I will hold you up and retain you with my victorious right hand of rightness and justice."* -Isaiah 41:10 AMP

While we were living in Puerto Rico, my father was pastoring a church, and my mother was an English professor at the University of Puerto Rico. Then, my parents, being visionaries and wanting to improve themselves, decided that they wanted to earn their doctorate degrees. They applied at several universities in the United States and were accepted at Indiana University, Bloomington Campus. So we rented our home in Puerto Rico and moved to Bloomington, Indiana for three years so they could earn their doctorate degrees.

When we arrived in Bloomington, it was time for me to start ninth grade at a brand new high school. I was very naive, shy, and insecure because it was a different environment and culture. In addition, the only language spoken was English, which was very different than when I lived in Puerto Rico.

I didn't know anyone, or have any friends, and no one spoke Spanish, so even though I understood and spoke English, I still had a lot of adjusting to do. I really felt out of place because all the students would look at us as if we were "aliens." Most of the students looked different than we did, and I had a feeling that *word* had gotten out that we were from Puerto Rico and that we possibly didn't know how to speak English.

I spoke Spanish so well that for my elective, I decided to take French since the Spanish class at the high school would have probably been boring and not challenging enough. I ended up taking French every year in high school. (I was even able to pass the Indiana University placement tests, both in Spanish and French, and got 10 college credits for each language.) Unfortunately, I didn't continue practicing my French and have now forgotten most of it. I am definitely thankful that I'm fluent with my Spanish language!

I recall there was a time, while in high school, that I had to get in front of my English class to give a speech. I felt overwhelmed about that assignment. When it was my turn, I fearfully walked up to the front of the room to speak and "froze." I remember feeling like I was from another planet as I looked at all the students staring at me with perplexed demeanors.

As I started to speak in my broken English, I was concerned that maybe they wouldn't understand me. I did the best I could with my heavy accented English and returned to my desk. I wasn't sure what my classmates were thinking, and I was afraid they would reject me even more. All I could think of was that I was definitely relieved that the experience was over!

Another occasion in which I was afraid to speak was a time when I was in a science class. The teacher was giving directions for a homework assignment. I was listening attentively but felt that I was not quite able to understand the assignment. I wanted to raise my hand and ask, but I was afraid and concerned of what others would think, so I didn't ask. I decided to wait and ask some classmates privately after the class. To my surprise, they also had the same questions and were also afraid to ask.

Situations like that happened a few times, so little by little, I got in the habit of asking, and I started to become more confident. I kept thinking that by me asking, I would also be helping others that might have had the same question, so it didn't bother me to ask, and at least I would have the answer to my personal concerns.

As the years passed, every time I had to say something or ask a question in a group, my heart would beat like a *horse in a race*. However, eventually, and through my actions of stepping out and *doing what I was afraid of*, I learned that *action overcomes fear*. In other words, if I was afraid of doing something, I would ask God to give me the courage and *do it afraid* (in other words to do it in spite of feeling fear). As I did, I slowly started to overcome the fear of speaking in public.

Thinking back, I would've *never* thought that I would overcome that fear and end up being confident when speaking in public. Since then, I have been on many committees, have been president of groups, have hosted a cable TV show, received awards, and spoken in front of thousands. I have also led and continue to lead Bible studies in English and in Spanish.

As the years have gone by, and now that I'm grown, I've completed a few assessments and found out that one of my God-given gifts is to be an exhorter, to encourage and empower people to action. Also, the more I learned about God's Word and His promises, the more I've seen that He doesn't want us to live in fear.

> God's Word *"For God did not give us a spirit of timidity (of cowardice or craven and cranking and fawning fear), but (He has given us a spirit) power and of love and of a calm and well-balanced mind and discipline and self-control."*
> -2 Timothy 1:7

Let's not let anything hold us back! We have God's power, love, and self-discipline living on the inside of each of us to overcome any fears in our life! One of the meanings I've heard of the acronym FEAR is *False Evidence Appearing Real*. Always remember that action cures fear, and the more you do something you're afraid of, the more courageous you will become!

The Bible teacher, Joyce Meyer, just recently wrote a book called *Do It Afraid*. In it she talks about how people can transform their fears to be more courageous by doing what they have to do even if they're afraid. She further explains that courageous people take action to do what the moment requires, no matter how they feel or what others think. As we keep trusting God in all we do, He will make us fearless and courageous!

Promises in God's Word to Overcome Fear:

"The Lord is my light and my salvation—whom shall I fear? The Lord is the stronghold of my life—of whom shall I be afraid?" -Psalm 27:1 NIV

"Be strong, do not fear, your God will come, he will come with vengeance, with divine retribution he will come to save you." -Isaiah 35:4

"Have I not commanded you? Be strong and courageous. Do not be afraid; do not be discouraged, for the Lord your God will be with you wherever you go." -Joshua 1:9

"They will have no fear of bad news; their hearts are steadfast, trusting in the Lord. Their hearts are secure, they will have no fear; in the end they will look in triumph on their foes." -Psalm 112:7–8

"I sought the Lord, and he answered me; he delivered me from all my fears." -Psalm 34:4

"Never will I leave you; never will I forsake you. So we say with confidence, the Lord is my helper; I will not be afraid. What can mere mortals do to me?" -Hebrews 13:5b–6

"I will never (under any circumstances) desert you (nor give you up nor leave you without support, nor will I in any degree leave you helpless), nor will I forsake or let you down or relax my hold on you (assuredly not)!" So we take comfort and are encouraged and confidently say, "The Lord is my helper (in time of need), I will not be afraid. What will man do to me?" -Hebrews 13:5b–6 AMP

Action—Chapter 3: Overcoming Fear With Faith

Applying God's Word: Isaiah 41:10; 2 Timothy 1:7; Psalm 27:1; Isaiah 35:4; Joshua 1:9; Psalm 112: 7–8; Psalm 34:4; Hebrews 13:5b–6

1. Is there a fear that you feel you have, that holds you back from things you'd like to do in life? Please explain.
2. How does it affect the way you live? Does it lead to anger, worry, anxiety, or an attempt to control others?
3. How would your life be different if you could overcome that fear?
4. What promises in God's Word could encourage you to step out in faith?
5. What actions could you start taking to overcome your fears and to start experiencing more freedom and peace in your life?

Chapter 4

Hungry for God's Word

God's Word: *"Blessed are those who hunger and thirst for righteousness, for they will be filled." -Matthew 5:6*

I attended high school in Bloomington, Indiana, while my parents were working on their Doctor of Philosophy degrees. As a family, we always attended a church in the city. However, I never really learned much about how to understand the Bible. It was a weekly routine, which I was used to, going through the motions of attending church and feeling good about it. I never really grasped the practical meaning or understanding of the Bible. I was always curious to know more and felt that there was something extra special about that book. I wanted to know more about it. I only learned certain portions, lessons, messages, and parts of the Bible, but never got a good solid understanding that I could grasp onto and apply to my life.

My parents completed their Ph.Ds at Indiana University in three years—my dad in Adult Education and my mom in Speech Communication and Public Speaking—and were ready to go back to Puerto Rico. I had just finished my junior year in high school, so instead of my parents taking me to finish my senior year in a new high school in Puerto Rico, they found out that I could get enough credits to graduate from high school in half of my senior year. I ended up living with one of my mother's friends in Bloomington and completed all my requirements to graduate from Bloomington High School North in three and a half years.

In December, I moved back to Puerto Rico to live with my family again. They were living on the campus of a Puerto Rican seminary near the University of Puerto Rico. My mom taught at the university, and my dad taught at the seminary. I always thought it was so special and cool that we lived at the seminary, because all the people there were interested in studying more about God's Word so they could teach others. I just wished I could've been learning more too.

While I lived in the seminary, since I had already completed high school, my mom was able to find a job for me at the University of Puerto Rico working as a receptionist in one of the offices. During that time, we were making arrangements for me to be accepted to Indiana University, so I could return to Bloomington and complete a Bachelor's degree.

During that semester, I will never forget a vivid memory. One evening I was sitting on the floor by the nightstand next to my bed reading the Bible. I was used to reading it every night, but that night was different. I remember looking up to heaven, with my Bible in my hands, and crying out to God, "I want to be able to learn, and understand this Bible, so I can teach others the Power of your Word!"

I had been taught and heard over and over how well-known and popular the Bible was, but I just didn't understand it! It was so overwhelming for me to try to figure out how to learn it! I was hoping and praying that someday I would be able to grasp its meaning and lessons, have a great relationship with God, and apply it to my life.

> God's Word: *"I will find the Lord when I seek him with all my heart and with all my soul."* -Deuteronomy 4:29 AMP

That summer, I was accepted to Indiana University, Bloomington campus in the Group Students' program for minorities. I moved back to Indiana to start my Bachelor's in Elementary Education. There, I was all alone and far from my family again, but I felt and knew that God was with me.

Now back in Bloomington, I wanted to be involved in learning the Bible, but I didn't want to go back to the church my parents had attended when I was in high school. I remember that when we attended I found it to be boring, and I had not learned or understood the Bible so that I would be able to live it's principles.

As I walked around and started becoming familiar with my new college campus, I noticed many different flyers and various invitations to student Bible study groups. Not knowing anyone, I wasn't sure which one to attend, so I kept asking God to lead me to a good one.

One day at the cafeteria, I sat at a table and a guy started talking with me. He told me about a Bible study that he attended in which they really taught a lot about the Bible and that he had learned more than he could ever imagine. He told me about a class they made available to him in which he learned amazing things. He said he was learning to finally be able to understand the Bible. I started getting excited about visiting his Bible study and learning more about God's Word, especially because of the way he was talking about it!

I started attending the Bible study and was eager to take the class to learn and understand the Bible better. For the very first time in my life I felt as if I was on top of the world with all the things I was learning! It was only a three-week class, but it taught me the basic keys in the Word of God from Genesis to Revelation to be able to understand how it all fits together. I definitely learned an amazing overview, perspective, and clear understanding about the purpose, value, benefits, and power of God's Word! My life was forever changed!

The key Bible verse of the class was *John 10:10 KJV*, *"The thief cometh not, but for to steal, and to kill, and to destroy; I am come that they may have life, and that they might have it more abundantly."* The perspective was that since Jesus came, we *"might have life, and have it more abundantly."* Why are there so many Christians not manifesting this more abundant life? The key was to study and rightly divide God's Word.

> God's Word: *"Study to shew thyself approved unto God, a workman that needeth not to be ashamed, rightly dividing the word of truth."* -2 Timothy 2:15

Not only did I learn the importance of studying God's Word but also how vital it is to understand the context of when it was written and to whom the messages apply. In addition, I was learning the value of renewing my mind to what God's Word says to believe and do so that I could prove what is His *"good, and acceptable and perfect will,"* and receive all His blessings *(Romans 12:2)*. I also found out how to tap into our God-given spiritual abilities (like having a sixth sense), to live that *more abundant life* that Jesus came to make available.

> God's Word: *"For the Word of God is alive and active. Sharper than any double-edged sword, it penetrates even to the dividing soul and spirit, joints and marrow, it judges the thoughts and attitudes of the heart."* -Hebrews 4:12 NIV

I learned that the greatest secret in the world today is that the Bible is the revealed Word and Will of God! It is the "manual of life," just as we need a manual to understand how things work, like our cell phones, TVs, cars, etc. If we want a great life, we need to read God's Word, the Bible, as our "Manual for Life." God's Word is valuable and powerful and has a purpose in our life!

God is the creator of life, and He has given us a book full of great and precious promises, as stated in *2 Peter 1:3–4*, *"His divine power has given us everything we need for a godly life through our knowledge of him who called us by his own glory and goodness. Through these he has given us his very great and precious promises, so that through them you may participate in the divine nature, having escaped the corruption in the world caused by evil desires!"*

Nowadays most people do not believe that the Bible is the Word and Will of God. They take out one segment of the Word of God and insert another. But to be logical, fair, and consistent, either the entire Bible is the Word of God from Genesis to Revelation, or it is not the Word of God anywhere. Knowing the Bible is the book of life and the Will of God for our life is a primary step in beginning to live a more abundant life, and living a victorious and fulfilling life.

I am so extremely thankful that God opened the doors for me to learn His Word and be spiritually fed because I was *starving* to know His Word. I have continued in that journey throughout my life. Things I learned then and have continued to experience in my life have helped me face all the challenges that I've had, knowing that He loves me and that I'm never alone!

Action—Chapter 4: Hungry for God's Word

Applying God's Word: Matthew 5:6; Deuteronomy 4:29; John 10:10; 2 Timothy 2:15; Romans 12:2; Hebrews 4:12; 2 Peter 1:3–4

1. Have you ever felt a need or desire to know and understand God's Word more?
2. What kind of topics would you like to learn more about?
3. Why is it important to study and to learn God's Word?
4. What have you done or where can you go to learn more about God's Word?
5. Can you list some resources that could be helpful as you start studying God's Word?

Chapter 5

Shining for God

> God's Word: *"Do everything without grumbling or arguing, so that you may become blameless and pure, children of God without fault in a warped and crooked generation. Then you will shine among them like stars in the sky as you hold firmly to the word of life."* Philippians 2:14–16a NIV

Throughout my years at Indiana University, I continued to study the Word of God. In the summer of 1975, I decided to participate in a program called Indiana Illuminators with the Bible study group I had joined. I was sent to Northwest Indiana with a group of women to live there for June and July, during our summer break. It was like a missionary program.

First we were to find a place to live, then find a job, and begin a small Bible study in our home. Then, we were to share God's Word with people in that area and encourage them to take the three-week Bible class. The ultimate goal was to empower them to start an intimate relationship with God and start living a more abundant life.

I never understood why, but being only 18 years old, I was chosen to be the leader of the four older women that were assigned to our group. There were many challenges that we faced that summer, which I had geared up for, but I never imagined trying to find a place to rent for only two months would be the very first one. Right from the beginning, we had to start building *spiritual muscles* by truly relying on God for our basic needs!

When we first arrived in our assigned city, we were invited to spend one week at some believer's home while we were waiting to find a place to live for the summer. Well, the week went by super fast, and we still hadn't found a place. The program's rule was that we had to move out of the home after that first week. The purpose of this rule was to help push us into action and to build our belief in God as our helper and provider.

It was the last day of our stay as guests in the home, and we still had not found a place to rent. I remember having all our luggage on the front lawn, and it was 5 p.m. on that June afternoon. We had looked everywhere ... what were we to do? As the leader of the group, I got the three other ladies into "brainstorming mode." We also intensely prayed to God to lead us to find a place by that evening. It truly seemed like an impossible feat at that moment!

While I paced back and forth trying to think of what to do, the other ladies sat on their suitcases which were on the lawn all depressed and wondering what we would do. At the same time, I was asking God for the courage and determination to find a place! I just couldn't see us sleeping on that lawn. Giving up was *not* an option.

Being desperate, I got inspired to go door to door knocking and asking the neighbors if they knew of a place for rent where we could move to and rent for two months. However, I had to be fearless and get into immediate action! One of the other ladies of our team wanted to accompany me to also see how God could answer our prayer!

I was fired up and urgently started speaking to God, "I don't know where you want us to go God, but I know you have a place for us. Please show us where you want us to live tonight! We are here to work for you, and we trust you, and thank you for providing for us!" That's the way I had learned to fight "spiritual battles," by speaking positive, hopeful, and thankful words out of my mouth boldly!

We were desperate and determined to find a place! I began to reflect and started confessing *Philippians 4:6 AMP*, which says, *"Do not fret or have any anxiety about anything, but in every circumstance and in everything, by prayer and petition (definite requests), with thanksgiving, continue to make your wants known to God."*

Another promise that I thought about was from *Proverbs 3:5–6 NIV*, "Trust in the Lord with all your heart and lean not on your own understanding; in all your ways submit to him, and he will make your paths straight"

It was already getting dark and I was down to the last house on the block. A lady answered the door, and I frantically told her our story. She was very moved and concerned for us. After giving it some thought, she suddenly said that she knew of an empty house that was a few blocks away. She said she knew who owned it and that they were trying to find a long-term renter. Nevertheless, since it was such an urgent situation she was willing to ask if we could live in the home *only* for the summer! She immediately made the phone call to her friend, and YES! We got the green light to go live in it! What an exciting miracle! And, as promised, God did provide!

We practically ran back to the lawn where the two other ladies were sitting watching our belongings and shared the awesome news! We immediately gathered in a circle to pray and praise God! It was already evening and dark outside, but we excitedly gathered our belongings with our hearts full of thankfulness to God who had led us there!

A verse from God's Word that had been working in my mind as we had been desperately searching for a place to live was *1 Peter 5:7 AMP*, "Casting the whole of your care, (all your anxieties, all your worries, all your concerns, once and for all), on Him, for he cares for you affectionately and cares about you watchfully."

The phrase "cast your care," is another way of saying "don't worry." However, we are not supposed to "cast our responsibility." That's why I didn't give up. I was doing everything I could think of to act on, and then I was trusting God that He would meet our needs.

That's how I came up with one of my favorite phrases, "Do your best, and let God do the rest!" Saying that has helped me to have the courage to do what I CAN do, and then to have peace to accept the things I can't change, because God is right there to make sure everything works together for our good. *(Romans 8:28 KJV)*

I believe that in those days, all the challenges we went through were the beginning of a season of spiritual growth for me. During that time I had the opportunity to really *shine for God*. It definitely was a "faith-building" summer, which helped me develop a strong foundation for who I was becoming at 18; a young believer wanting to know more of God ... by experience! After that summer, God had continued to build my determination, and my trust in Him grew!

After that summer experience, I went back to Bloomington and continued to attend Indiana University for my sophomore year. I was very involved in teaching home Bible studies and continued to participate in different classes to learn more about God's Word. It sure was an exciting year! I had a lot of dreams and visions to spread God's Word throughout the world!

God's Word shows us of the kind of attitude we are encouraged to have during difficult times in *James 1:2–4, "Consider it pure joy, my brothers and sisters, whenever you face trials of many kinds, because you know that the testing of your faith produces perseverance. Let perseverance finish its work so that you may be mature and complete, not lacking anything."* This reminds me of a phrase I like to say, "When life gives you lemons, make lemonade!" And always remember that God is always with us, and as we wait on His timing, He will always lead us to victory!

Action—Chapter 5: Shining for God!

Applying God's Word: Philippians 2:14–16a; Philippians 4:6-7; Proverbs 3:5-6; I Peter 5:6-9; Romans 8:28; James 1:2–3

1. What is a challenge that you've been through which seemed impossible that things would work out, but you didn't give up, and it was resolved?
2. What should be the first thing we do when faced with a difficult situation?
3. What is the purpose and ultimate goal of prayer?
4. Which one of God's promises above encourages you the most?
5. How can we keep *shining for God* while we're going through challenges?

Chapter 6

Living for God in Everyday Life

God's Word: *"Preach the word, be prepared in season and out of season, correct, rebuke, and encourage, with great patience and careful instruction."* -2 Timothy 4:2

Making a Difference With My Family

While I was in college in Bloomington, Indiana, I met a young man that was very much interested in the Bible studies and also in me. He was studying to be a doctor, and my parents knew him and thought he would be a great candidate for me to marry. I didn't feel quite ready, but I felt I would have a secure and good future with him. We got married in August 1976. I was only 19 years old and starting my junior year at Indiana University.

We lived on Bloomington campus at Indiana University (IU), but then the next year, moved to Northwest Indiana, since he had finished his doctorate. I was able to complete my senior year at IU Northwest in 1978 and graduated with a Bachelor's degree in Elementary Education, with a Multicultural Education Endorsement.

Shortly after buying our first home in Hammond, Indiana, I was hired and started teaching in Northwest Indiana in the East Chicago School System. Then in 1981 we moved to a home in Munster, Indiana, which was about 20 minutes from the Hammond home. While teaching and starting our family, I also took more classes, and in 1983, I completed a Master's in Elementary Education with a Bilingual Endorsement.

Throughout my teaching career I mainly taught third grade with Spanish as a second language. I loved God and always applied His principles to encourage and motivate children by always *catching* them doing good things and acknowledging them. They enjoyed all the recognition, and the result was that most of them wanted to behave and to improve their work. My students were very happy and loved coming to school. I continued teaching until the year 2000.

Between 1979 and 1988, within 10 years, I gave birth to five beautiful and healthy children: Melisa, Elena, Selina, Cristina, and Tony! They brought me tremendous joy and I treasured being their mom. At the same time it was an extremely busy time in my life, raising the five children and teaching school full time.

Even though it was overwhelming, one of the reasons why I was able to keep teaching was because we were able to have some family and friends as live-in babysitters when the children were young. That helped for a few years, but it was a challenge keeping up with all the many other household responsibilities such as cleaning, grocery shopping, cooking, managing the finances, and making sure all my children's needs were met, as well as working full-time. In addition, as a teacher, there were always papers to grade, and things to do to prepare for school, not only for me, but also my five children.

We attended Bible studies as a family, and raised our children with the knowledge of God, learning his Word and teaching them how to pray. I remember that I would come home from teaching all day and would go straight to the kitchen still wearing my high heels to cook a full dinner. Even though it was a sacrifice, one of my favorite memories was when all seven of us sat at our oval kitchen table, prayed over the meal, and had a delicious dinner together catching up on the events of the day.

I vividly remember the times I was with my five children in the grocery store and we had to use two carts, one for the food and the other for my two younger children Crissy and Tony. As we would go down the aisles Melisa, Elena, and Selina would help me find the food and were marvellous helpers. People would see us and ask, "How do you do it?" All I could think of to say was, "I don't know, I just do it." I didn't have much of a choice since things had to get done. As I look back, that season of my life was insurmountable and stressful trying to manage work, family, and everything else I chose to get involved in.

As a family, we did our best to have a fun life, go on vacations, and spent quality time together. We were also able to expose our children to many activities—from sports, to dance classes, learning musical instruments, being Girl Scouts, many school activities, birthday parties, and to having fun with their friends. It was quite a challenge figuring out our weekly schedules, but we were able to make it work by always using calendars and charts to track various household chores. We were a very industrious family!

I believe what kept me going and doing what needed to be done was having God in my life. I sensed that He was always with me and would help me. I realize now that one of the ways that I coped with all the pressure of what I "had" to do, was to get involved in things I could "choose" to do. They were still more work, but seemed like "fun" activities, as I felt that I was helping others, feeling appreciated, and making a positive difference for God.

In retrospect, I wish that I could turn back time and that I would've spent more quality time with my children and been more involved in their activities, and more present in their lives. I was aware that they would grow up one day and felt that I was being there for them. In my heart I was doing the best that I could at that time. But, I also sensed that I was going through the motions being busy and just "existing". As I reflect on this today, I realized that I was connecting my value to all the things I was doing. I have regrets and I wish I could go back in time and have all five of them young again... but I must forgive myself, as God saw my heart and forgives me.

Even though our family was not perfect...who's is?, and we had our struggles, I am thankful to God that our five children have grown up as honest, hardworking and successful adults. My prayer is that God protects them, guides them, keeps them healthy, and that they will always know how proud I am of them, and the deep and unending love that God and I have for each of them!

God's Word: *"That the generation to come might know them, that the children still to be born might arise and recount them to their children. That they might set their hope in God and not forget the works of God but might keep His commandments."*
-Psalm 78:6-7

I learned that in life, whatever children are exposed to has an effect on them for the rest of their lives. Starting with being exposed to learning about God, and also our manner of living and life changing decisions we make for them and with them.

One example was the summer in which the three older girls were going to try new musical instruments with the school band program just for a three month period. Melisa wanted to try a saxophone, Elena a trumpet, and Selina a clarinet. We went to the school band room to rent the instruments.

Elena and Selina easily got the instruments they wanted. However, when Melisa asked about the saxophone, the music director had her try to blow into a mouth piece to make a sound. But since it was the first time that she had ever tried it, the sound didn't come out right. Immediately, she was told that she should learn the trombone instead, because it would be easier. We weren't convinced, but since it was only for the summer, we went ahead and rented it, along with the trumpet and the clarinet.

As we walked out to the car, I could tell Elena and Selina were really excited about their instruments, but I observed that Melisa was a little disappointed because her expectations had been on learning how to play a saxophone. I also started to feel a little bothered that the band director didn't give her the opportunity to try the instrument she had dreamed about and was expecting to try. I had a gut feeling that *something* had to be done.

At that moment, I had a decision to make—should I just go home and have her try the trombone for three months and then try the saxophone at another time? Or, should I go back into the school and insist that they give her the opportunity to try the saxophone for the three months? I started thinking that since we had to pay for the rental anyway, why shouldn't we be able to choose the instrument she *really* wanted?

I felt a little embarrassed, but we walked back into the school and assertively requested that she be given a saxophone to rent for the summer instead of the trombone. Without hesitation, they agreed and gave Melisa the saxophone! She was thrilled, and I was so glad we decided to go back and that we got the instrument she really wanted!

The reason why I wanted to share this story is because the results from that decision at that moment have lasted a lifetime. Melisa went on to be one of the top senior musicians in her competitive class and won local, regional, and state competitions playing the saxophone. In addition, she received a scholarship to college and earned a Bachelor's Degree in Musical Theater and Performance from Indiana University, which is one of the top music schools in the world. She's performed in New York City, Chicagoland, and throughout the state of Indiana, and to this day continues to play her saxophone! (https://www.facebook.com/melisa.mccann.music/)

I believe that all these accomplishments were the fruit of the decision we made THAT DAY when we turned back to get her *dream instrument*—the saxophone! Everything we do in life is like seeds we plant ... sooner or later we will reap what we sow! I have learned that we must use wisdom and realize that in the long run our choices and decisions have positive, or negative, long term results in life.

We are also examples to our children, and things we do and say have an effect in their lives forever. No matter all the ups and downs, disappointments, and frustrations we went through, I am proud and thankful to say that our five children have gone to college, have attained degrees, and have productive and successful lives! I give God All the Glory!

> God's Word: *"And let us not lose heart and grow weary and faint in acting nobly and doing right, for in due time and at the appointed season we shall reap, if we do not loosen and relax our courage and faint." -Galatians 6:9 AMP*

Making a Difference in My Community

> God's Word: *"Have I not commanded you? Be strong and courageous. Do not be afraid; do not be discouraged, for the Lord your God will be with you wherever you go." -Joshua 1:9 NIV*

Throughout the years of raising my five children and teaching school, I also loved to be involved in our community. It was my time to socialize with adults and to make a positive difference in the community.

I once attended an event for community leaders in someone's house, and an announcement was made that a cable TV station needed a volunteer to host a TV show called "East Chicago Presents." I noticed that no one volunteered, so I built up the courage to privately walk up to the producers to ask them some questions.

After the men explained and answered my questions, I thought that it would be a good experience and a marvelous opportunity to get to know more people in the community and spread positive news. I also believed it would be fun to acquire knowledge and experience in the TV industry.

The program was like an interview setting in which I would invite guests and ask a variety of questions about their careers, their services, and their involvement in the community. It turned out to be a wonderful experience to interview doctors, dentists, attorneys, politicians, teachers, school principals, store owners, community leaders, beauty pageant contestants, and even my own amazing parents. Even though it was a lot of work and a challenging volunteer experience, it was very fulfilling.

After a few months doing the 30-minute weekly programs on Tuesday nights at 7 p.m., since I was the only one inviting guests, the producers suggested that we would call it "The Ruth Benavente Show"! By going through this experience, without me realizing it, God was working in me to build courage since I was totally out of my comfort zone, at least at the beginning. Throughout the two year experience, I became more confident and very interested in all the different things that people do to help others. It was another opportunity to practice the lesson that *action overcomes fear!*

Making a Difference With Women

> God's Word: *"Be strong and courageous. Do not be afraid or terrified because of them, for the Lord your God goes with you; he will never leave you nor forsake you."* -Deuteronomy 31:6

In the community of East Chicago where I taught elementary school, the population was mainly Hispanics and minorities. There were many Hispanic teachers and professionals as well. Besides being involved in the cable TV show, I got involved with a group of professional Hispanic women who were interested in being mentors to other young Hispanic high school girls. They decided to start a group called the Hispanic Women's Forum (HWF) of Northwest Indiana.

The main goal of the group was to encourage young ladies, and especially their Hispanic parents, to continue their education past high school and to reach for their dreams. (The reason why we took this approach was because in the Hispanic culture a lot of times young ladies were overprotected and sometimes not allowed to go away to college or to seek additional education after high school.)

The HWF group's main annual event was a mother-daughter luncheon in which we invited all the Senior Hispanic young ladies from the two East Chicago High Schools. At the event, we would all contribute a dish, have a special keynote speaker, and do a raffle for a $300 scholarship. The young lady who won it would get to apply her winnings towards her future studies. It was a very beautiful and encouraging event, which the mothers and daughters were very grateful for. Our group also appreciated the opportunity to serve as Hispanic role models and to encourage them to build their dreams!

I continued to stay involved with the HWF group for several years and was eventually elected to be the president of the group. I held that position for about five years. During the time that I was president, one of my goals was to find a way that we could expand the mother-daughter luncheons to include more cities and school systems in our metropolitan area, as there were also Hispanics in those areas.

The problem was that we didn't have the funds to be able to do anything much larger than the event we were holding at the elementary school cafeteria. Another thing some of the members wanted to do was to be able to include our own Hispanic daughters so that they would also be able to be involved and participate in the extra special mother-daughter luncheons.

My desire was to come up with something to do about that challenge.

I recall one of the monthly meetings that I was presiding over where the mother-daughter event was being discussed. All of a sudden, out of *nowhere,* I got a *bright idea* that we should expand the luncheon. I shared my idea to expand the event to include all the Hispanic high school seniors of other cities in our metropolitan area. Obviously we would need more funds to be able to do that, so I suggested that maybe we could start an annual dinner-dance fundraiser.

We had never done a dinner-dance before, so this was a totally new concept, and it seemed that it was completely out of our reach to try to hold two big events during the year—a fundraiser, and a mother-daughter luncheon. However, something inside of me was up to that difficult task. I *could* visualize it, and I believed we could make it work!

Almost immediately, the ladies at the meeting looked at me as if I was out of my mind! They knew this would require an overwhelming amount of work and dedication. Just about all of them had a negative comment or were shaking their heads saying that the idea was ridiculous and impossible for a small group of women like ours to take on. I started to feel like my parade was being rained on and that my vision for growth and expansion of the group was being shattered! They were so against it that they didn't even want me to explain any details about how I was thinking it might work.

I totally felt out of place and like I didn't belong there. I quickly gathered all the paperwork in front of me, put it in my briefcase, stood up, and said, "That's okay we don't have to do any of this. I'll just take my energy and ideas, and go somewhere else to make a difference." As I started to leave, the ladies were shocked! They looked at me and asked me to stop and to please stay and share my ideas. I did. They listened attentively and decided to try to make it work at least for one year.

I am so proud to say that with God's help and guidance I was able to lead our group of about 20 women to hold our first HWF Fundraiser Dinner-Dance and raised thousands of dollars, which allowed us the opportunity to reach out to all the high schools in Northwest Indiana!

We were able to invite all the Senior Hispanic females and their mothers to our new and expanded HWF Annual Mother-Daughter Luncheon. After that, we were also able to hold the luncheons at a very elegant restaurant. In addition, we held essay contests to provide several thousands of dollars for scholarships to the young Hispanic girls! It was a lot of work, but it was worth it! And thanks to God, His vision, and wisdom, we were able to make a positive impact on hundreds of lives for many years!

Making a Difference With the Students

> God's Word: *"You are my hiding place; you will protect me from trouble and surround me with songs of deliverance."*
> -Psalm 32:7

As an elementary school teacher in East Chicago, Indiana, for about 20 years, I mainly taught in a third grade bilingual classroom. That meant that I was in a regular third grade classroom, however I also taught Spanish as a second language.

In addition, since we were a bilingual classroom, children who wanted to learn Spanish as a second language and also children that came from other Hispanic speaking countries who did not speak English were also placed in my classroom. That way, I could teach them English, as well as all the other subjects, in a way they could understand. This was an extremely challenging teaching situation to manage every day.

As a third grade teacher, I was required to teach language arts, which includes Spelling, Language, and Reading (I had three different levels). I also had to teach Math, Science, Social Studies, and two levels of Spanish (basic beginner and advanced). In addition, we had to teach our own Art, Music, and Gym classes.

To prepare for my classes, I had to have weekly pre-planned lesson plans for every subject, for every hour of the day. In addition to everything that I was teaching, there were many papers to grade, plus all the excuses and disciplinary situations

I had to deal with. We were also expected to communicate with the parents regarding their children's individual progress or needs, especially if there were problems.

Even though I taught school in East Chicago, I lived in the city of Munster where my five children went to school. In Munster, the school children were predominantly Caucasian, and I would notice that the whole school culture and manner in which they did things was different.

I started to observe that at my children's school, they had special teachers that would teach Art, Music, and Gym. During that time, computers were also coming out, and they had a computer lab in the school where the children would go learn how to use computers. My school system didn't have any special teachers or a computer lab.

I began comparing the differences between my children's school and the school where I taught. Besides the school system where I taught not having special teachers to teach Art, Music, and Gym, we also didn't have a computer lab, Social Studies books, or teacher's editions, and in the Science books that we had, "man" had not landed on the moon (and this was in the 80s). Textbooks, the basic learning tool of any school, were outdated in the school where I taught, and I found this disturbing!

As time went on, I started asking questions to other teachers, my immediate supervisors, and principals. I even went to a meeting at the school board building and addressed my concerns to the school superintendent. During the meeting, they invited people to ask questions. I walked up to the microphone in a room full of people, and with God's help, dared to ask the question about the discrepancies and lack of basic materials. The superintendent looked at me and uncaringly said, "If you don't like what we have and how we do things around here, why don't you go find a job somewhere else?"

What a shock! It felt like it was a slap in the face! I was speechless! That was so disrespectful to me and all the minority children in our school system! Something inside me rose up, and I felt I had to DO something besides "finding a job somewhere else." I had to stand up for the children and all the parents that were helpless and at the mercy of how the school system's leaders were limiting their children's education.

I had also heard that the school system was one of the richest in the whole metropolitan area, in other words, they had more money per student than other systems, including where my children went to school. So what was happening? Where was the money going or being spent? Apparently it was not being spent to hire proper Art, Music, and Gym teachers and to provide computers, Social Studies books, or updated Science books for children to learn!

After praying about the whole situation, I felt deep down that the parents were the main ones who had the right to know what was really going on and to complain, as it affected *their own* children. In addition, their tax money was supposed to be used to educate their children in the best way possible.

So I decided that I would invite my students' parents to my classroom after school and share my concerns. They were all shocked and perplexed about the situation as well! They wanted to know if and how they could make a difference. So we organized a plan to find out and compare all the school systems in the area to see how our school system compared to all the others.

A chart was put together, which included the categories of Art, Music, and Gym teachers, computer labs, and whether they had Social Studies and Science books. Then calls were made and the summary report was completed from all the school systems in the area.

The parents became energized and empowered to find out more about what was happening in their school system and to their children. They started to tell other parents, who also became concerned about what was going on in their school system. Soon they started a formal group and decided to call themselves the East Chicago Concerned Parents. Then they went to a community organization called the United Citizens Organization (UCO) to share their findings and concerns.

The UCO was extremely disturbed and was determined to find answers to why the school system was lacking in so many needed and essential learning books, computers, and teachers.

They held a huge community meeting in which they invited the school superintendent. They set up a chair for him in the front of the room with his name on it so they could ask him questions. However, he never showed up to address the community's concerns.

The very next day, since the area newspaper media was also at the meeting, they wrote an article in the front page of the local newspaper. They addressed the situation about the children in East Chicago lacking in educational materials and in special teachers. The word kept getting out, and then the Chicago TV news media decided to come to East Chicago and find out what was going on. They first visited the administration building, where they were told that all the schools had everything they needed and that the parents were making things up.

After that, the Chicago TV news media contacted the UCO community organization, who knew that I was the teacher that had organized the parents. Then the TV media decided they had to specifically speak with me to get to the root of the story. So on the morning of March 23, 1988 (and 3 months pregnant with my fifth child Tony!), the TV news vans pulled up in front of my school looking for me.

I was in my classroom, when unexpectedly, a lady from the community organization entered the school through the side entrance and went up to the second floor where I was, with my teacher's aide and all my students. She frantically explained to me that the TV media was outside in front of the school building and that I needed to go down to speak with them, because the school system was denying the story about the needed materials and special teachers.

I was definitely startled and caught off track! To make it worse, asking the front office for permission to step out was not an option because I suspected they would not allow me to go speak with the media. So I nervously pondered, "Should I go outside and probably get in trouble?"

The lady kept insisting that they had to speak with me or else all our work would've been in vain. So I decided that *this was the moment* when I could express the reality of the situation and be heard, and that maybe *something* could be done to help the children. I decided to walk outside and talk to the TV media.

I left my students with my teacher aide and walked downstairs through the side door of the building. I saw the TV vans, reporters, and microphones waiting for me at the front of the building. As I slowly walked towards the vans on the sidewalk in front of the three story school building, I felt that everyone was looking out the windows wondering what was going on. It was like a "slow-motion" walk for me in my mind.

Besides thinking about all the trouble I could get into, and maybe even getting fired, more importantly, I was thinking about ALL the students, parents, and lives that *could be changed* by me speaking out. At that moment, as I was walking towards the TV vans, I confidently looked up to heaven and prayed, "God I know this is crazy, but someone has to speak up for these students, parents, and community organizers. Something is not right in this city. So even if I get fired, it will be worth it, because I know and feel that YOU ARE with me!"

It was like an *Esther 4:14* moment ("for such a time as this ...") in which I had to put everything on the line for what I truly believed in, trusting that God was with me. I felt in my heart that He would take care of me for doing the right thing.

When I arrived by the vans, I was interviewed by the TV reporter for about 15 minutes. I confirmed that the information they had was correct and that something needed to be done to improve the education in our school system.

After the interview, I walked back to the side of the building and quickly ran up the stairs to my classroom on the second floor. I was definitely shaken about what had just happened and started to get concerned about the negative consequences that I might confront. I kept praying and asking God to help me deal with whatever would occur.

The day continued as normal, but at the end of the day when I went to clock out at the office, there was a letter in my school teacher mailbox. It was from my principal. My heart started beating very fast, and I nervously opened it. The letter stated that it was noted that I had left the building and had left my students unattended (which was not true because I had a teacher's aide). It also said that I needed to give a written explanation of why I had left the building, and that I needed to respond in writing within 48 hours. In the letter, there was no mention about the TV vans or news media out in front of the building. I was certain that it was the reason why I had received the letter.

My thoughts were all over the place, and my heart began to pound as I was deciding what to write. I was pondering about how to explain my actions without explaining the whole situation behind why I had *really* left the classroom. I immediately became quiet and asked God how I should proceed and who would be able to help me with this dilemma.

> God's Word: *"The Lord is a refuge for the oppressed, a stronghold in times of trouble. Those who know your name trust in you, for you, Lord, have never forsaken those who seek you"*
> -Psalm 9:9 NIV

I didn't have any teachers that were willing to stand with me on these issues, even though they knew the truth of the situation. I was on my own. Even my teacher friends had already mentioned to me that they didn't want to be involved and that this whole thing might *blow up in my face*. There it was … blowing up!

I continued to think about what I had done, but I didn't seem to mind, because to me, it was the principle of the matter, and children's lives were being affected in a negative way. I had felt that they were innocent and helpless. It was up to me to stand up for them, and their parents, and even more so, for all the minorities represented in that school system. There was something inside of me *driving me*. Throughout the whole process, I kept trusting God and the promises that I had learned about fairness and justice.

As soon as I left the building that afternoon, I decided to contact my teachers' union representative concerning the situation and how to respond to the principal's letter. She told me she had to check with the union attorneys to find out about what I might be facing and about how I should respond to the letter from my principal. The attorneys were not able to get back in touch with me within the timeframe that the principal had given me, so I ended up having to write the response myself, with God's help.

As I wrote my response to the principal, I kept it very simple. I emphasized that I had not left my students alone, that they were with a teacher's aide, and that I had to step out of the classroom briefly, but came right back. I didn't mention anything about the TV news media or vans, since he hadn't mentioned it in his letter to me either. I took my response to him within the 48 hours. He waited a few days and then finally notified me that he wanted me to meet him in his office after school.

When I went to the principal's office, as he had requested, he told me that the punishment for leaving the classroom and walking outside of the school building would be that I would be suspended without pay for two days. I was devastated and felt that the punishment was really a retaliation for me speaking to the media. On prior occasions, myself and other teachers had also left the building to get something from their car, and there was no punishment imposed. So why did he decide to punish me this time and in this manner?

The word got out that I had been suspended for two days, and *The Times Newspaper* printed an article on May, 5, 1988 on the front page entitled, "School Suspends Teacher." It explained why I was suspended for two days for addressing the fact that, based on a 15-school survey comparing the Lake County school systems, the children in East Chicago lagged far behind other systems in providing materials, books, and certain classes. It seemed ridiculous that it had gotten to this point, and I was embarrassed to have been suspended, but at the same time I was glad I took the opportunity to stand up for justice, and I was very thankful to God that I didn't lose my job.

> God's Word: *"Righteousness and justice are the foundation of your throne; love and faithfulness go before you. Blessed are those who have learned to acclaim you, who walk in the light of your presence, Lord." -Psalm 89:14*

Action—Chapter 6: Living for God in Everyday Life

Applying God's Word: 2 Timothy 4:2; Psalm 78:6-7; Galatians 6:9; Joshua 1:9; Deuteronomy 31:6; Psalms 32:7; Esther 4:14; Psalm 9:9; Psalm 89:14

1. Do you believe that God wants to have a relationship with you everyday or just on Sundays?
2. Have you experienced any situations in which you have gotten into "good trouble" by following your heart to do the "right thing"?
3. In what areas of your life would you like to see changes and experience God's power?
4. What will the result of having God be more involved in your daily life mean to you?
5. Which of the Bible verses above would help strengthen you from the inside out?

Chapter 7

Divine Promotions

God's Word: *"For as the heavens are higher than the earth, so are my ways higher than your ways and my thoughts than your thoughts." -Isaiah 55:9*

Everything went fairly back to normal with my everyday school activities after my two day school suspension and the front page article in the newspaper. We finished the school year and enjoyed our two-month summer vacation.

However, when the teachers returned back to school, I started to see some changes. I noticed that we were provided new updated Science and Social Studies books, a new computer lab in our school, and the administration started hiring Art, Music, and Gym teachers!

So all the work the parents, the community organization, and the daring actions I took ended up creating good outcomes! And the best part was that the students would benefit by receiving a better quality education! As far as I was concerned, the results were worth all the risks and inconvenience!

I thought all the dust had settled, but God was not done with His plans. A few months later in the fall season, I received a call from an attorney in the area that had read and saved the front page article that had come out in the newspaper in May from when I had been suspended.

He shared with me that he was impressed with how I stood up for all the students' needs and even put my job on the line to speak out for them to have well-deserved, needed, and proper materials and education. The attorney continued to say that he thought of me when he found out that the Governor of Indiana was looking to appoint two additional citizens to the Indiana Civil Rights Commission Board.

The State Board was composed of seven people throughout the state of Indiana, and at this time they had two vacancies to fill. He said he thought that I would be a great candidate to recommend because of my dedication, integrity, and character. He also mentioned that the state had never had a Hispanic serve on that commission and that this would be a good opportunity for the governor to assign the first one.

After going through the application and review process, I was appointed by Governor Evan Bayh as the first Hispanic Civil Rights Commissioner for the State of Indiana in October 1989. The commission's role was to enforce the civil rights laws of the state and investigate complaints of discrimination on people's rights and responsibilities under the Indiana Civil Rights Laws. An article came out in the *Indianapolis Recorder* newspaper with the announcement on November 4, 1989.

It was amazing how God had made a way for this *troublemaker teacher* to be appointed to that position! I definitely felt it was a *divine promotion*. Interestingly enough, the position would require me to participate in two-day monthly meetings in Indianapolis, Indiana, which was a three-hour drive from my home in Northwest Indiana. All of us seven commissioners would review legal documents of statewide complaints and vote on decisions that would uphold the state laws.

Through this *divine promotion,* God confirmed to me that He had been "proud" of me for standing up for the helpless children in the school system. Even though I had been punished by being suspended without pay for two days by my school system, I felt that God had granted me His *favor* and promoted me to be an Indiana Civil Rights Commissioner, to confirm that I had done the right thing!

> God's Word: *"Surely, Lord, you bless the righteous; you surround them with your favor as with a shield." -Psalm 5:12*

The other way God showed me that He was on my side, and to show His justice, was that the school system ended up paying me for the two days they had suspended me. In addition, they also paid me two days per month while I was in Indianapolis, since I was considered to be on an official civil duty leave and excused from my teaching responsibilities. This continued not only for one, but two terms, a total of eight years!

During that time, I had the privilege of defending people who had experienced injustice and discrimination on a state-wide level! That was such a blessing and a sign from God that His ways and plans are much higher and better than ours. And that we will be rewarded as we do our best to follow His ways!

> God's Word: *"Without faith it is impossible to please God, because anyone who comes to him must believe that he exists and that he rewards those who earnestly seek him." -Hebrews 11:6*

Due to all my involvement in the school as a teacher, with parents, the community, the Hispanic Women's Forum of Northwest Indiana, and the Indiana Civil Rights Commission, I was invited to participate at the 10th Anniversary of the United Steelworkers of America's Celebration.

The keynote speaker at the event was going to be the well-known Cesar Chavez, the President of United Farmworkers of America. I was honored to be asked to sit by Cesar Chavez! He was such a humble, but fearless man, who had made such a huge difference for thousands of farmworkers. It was almost like sitting by a "Mother Teresa," quiet and humble, but powerful. I felt honored by God to have had such an unexpected eye-opening experience.

> God's Word: *"Humble yourselves therefore under the mighty hand of God that he may exalt you in due time."*
> *-1 Peter 5:6 KJV*

Later that summer, to my surprise, I was also asked to participate on the board of the United States Hispanic Leadership Institute (USHLI) as a committee member. The USHLI had been having conferences for 20 years. That year, they were planning to hold a three-day annual conference in Chicago. It was attended by about 5,000 Hispanics, who came from all over the United States. I volunteered with them for several years by being on coordinating and organizing committees and assisting during the event.

One evening, at one of the dinners, I was sitting at the back of the huge and elegant ballroom. There were hundreds of tables and a 25-person head table. At the dinners they always had a pastor that would give the invocation. That specific night the pastor didn't show up, so the president of the USHLI, knowing that I was a Christian, decided to call my name over the microphone of the ballroom and asked if I would please go to the head table to pray for the dinner.

I was sitting and talking with the people at our table, so I didn't even hear him say my name when he made the announcement. Then someone told me that they had called my name and that they wanted me to go to the head table for a word of prayer before the meal. I was shocked but at the same time honored because I knew God was with me. I was confident that He would give me the words to bless the food, the conference, and the people. That was a very humbling experience in which I was proud to specifically represent God in that manner at the conference.

A few years later, in October of 1999, I was selected by the USHLI to receive one of the five awards that were given at the conference each year. I was awarded the William C. Velasquez Volunteer of the Year Award. During this event on that evening, I had the honor to be one of the 25 people sitting at the head table for the dinner. The ballroom was filled with approximately three thousand attendees. It was like a sea of wall to wall people.

After the dinner, we were asked to accept the award and share some words. I was very nervous when it was my time to speak, but I trusted that God would be with me as I spoke from my heart.

The next evening of the conference, one of the keynote speakers was the President of the United States, Bill Clinton. As part of the honors of being selected, the five award recipients, along with other leaders, had the privilege of sitting on the platform where the president was going to speak.

When the president was introduced, he came out and shook everyone's hand, including mine! It was a privilege, and part of me felt like I was truly God's ambassador, and it reminded me of 2 *Corinthians 5:20a NIV*, *"We are therefore Christ's ambassadors, as though God were making his appeal through us. We implore you on Christ's behalf: be reconciled to God."* We definitely represent God everywhere we go, all for His glory!

I've learned that no matter what experiences, risks, and challenges we go through in life, they are *tests* and *hurdles* to help strengthen us. They help us build our *spiritual muscles*, our faith, and our character. They are opportunities to hold onto God and His promises, and to trust Him no matter how dark or hopeless the situations may be.

God will never let us down! He created us and has a plan and purpose for our life. He will also guide us to all kinds of promotions and give us *favor* that sometimes we can't even dream or imagine!

> <u>God's Word:</u> *"Now unto him that is able to do exceeding abundantly above all that we ask, or think, according to the power that worketh in us, Unto him be glory in the church by Christ Jesus throughout all ages, world without end. Amen."*
> *-Ephesians 3:20 KJV*

Action—Chapter 7: Divine Promotions

Applying God's Word: Isaiah 55:9; Psalm 5:12; Hebrews 11:6; 1 Peter 5:6; Proverbs 3:5–6; 2 Corinthians 5:20a; Ephesians 3:20

1. Have you ever been in a situation in which it seemed that you had gotten in trouble but ended up being promoted? Please explain.
2. What kind of thoughts and attitudes should we have for God to promote us?
3. What's one promise in God's Word that you can confess that will keep you strong through difficulties and lead you to victory?
4. Why is it important to always follow your heart and trust God?

Chapter 8

A New Beginning

God's Word: *"To everything there is a season, and a time for every matter or purpose under heaven."* -Ecclesiastes: 3:1

I was married to the father of my five children for 20 years, and we had both been successful in many areas of our lives. We had a beautiful home, productive careers, and we both loved our children very much. We definitely had a lot of activities going on between all seven of us, but we managed to make things work.

However, I sensed something was missing in my married life. I felt that I was just *existing*. I was working in and out of the home, and in the community...but still I felt alone, even though I knew that God was with me. I came to realize that through all the busyness of life, I was escaping the reality that I was not truly fulfilled in my marriage.

My husband and I experienced difficulties with communication, finances, intimacy, respect, and trust—as other married couples do. We struggled for a few years and were growing apart. What was keeping us together was our five children, and my hope that someday things would change, but they didn't. Then, unfortunately our marriage ended in divorce in 1998.

I kept teaching in East Chicago, but moved out of our four bedroom home in Munster. I bought a townhouse in the same town that I could afford on one salary, then did my best keeping up with all my other debt and expenses. This transition was very challenging and sad, but at the same time I felt I had a fresh start in my life. I appreciated having more control over my decisions, and more peace.

Ever since I had lived in Northwest Indiana, every winter my family would visit Sarasota, Florida where my parents, my two brothers, David and Danny, and my sister Mimi lived. I was the only one from our immediate family that didn't live in Sarasota.

To encourage me to move down and show me their support, my parents had purchased a home, which was being rented while I decided if, and when, I was going to move down. I wanted to move to Florida, but there never seemed to be a good time. Being able to move there sounded like a dream for me.

In the winter of December 1999, as I was driving on my way to the airport, there was a blizzard on the highway. The snow was so thick that I could barely see the front hood of my car. Immediately, I imagined myself driving down a highway in Florida with palm trees along the sides and a completely clear view of where I was going. At that very moment, I made the decision that I was going to find out what it would take to find a job in Florida and move down.

After all, I already had a house waiting for me, and all I needed was a job! So why not? I had already been living in Indiana for 25 years and was definitely tired of cold winters and snow, and was ready for warm weather and palm trees! I was ready for a new beginning! I was determined to look into finding out what it would take to teach in Florida.

When I arrived in the Sunshine State, I was so excited to let my parents know that I had decided I was going to look into getting a job in Sarasota so I could finally move down. They were extremely happy, however, they told me that a few weeks earlier, they had made a decision to list the home they had bought for me for sale. I immediately thought, "Oh no!" Wow, what timing! It sure is a good thing that I was determined to find a job in Sarasota *that* Christmas!

My parents explained that they weren't sure if I would ever move and that they needed the money to buy another property for their retirement. They thought about how they could still work around the situation, and caused them a little bit of a financial challenge, but they did not mind taking the home off the market. They did all they could and found a way to take my future home off the market and still be able to purchase their retirement home. They were definitely looking forward to me moving to Sarasota!

We all enjoyed that Christmas of 2000 together having fun in the sun. After New Year's Day, since I was still in Sarasota, I decided to go in person to the School Board of Sarasota offices. I wanted to find out what it would take for me to get a teaching job in Sarasota. I immediately completed the application and submitted it to the Human Resources Department.

Since I was going to be leaving back to Indiana in the next couple of days, they decided to interview me right away. I was shocked to hear them ask me if I was ready to start teaching the next week, after the winter break. Of course I was not ready to start the next week, but I accepted the offer and told them that I'd make arrangements to start in the fall semester. Wow, what an open door and a sign from God that the timing was just right!

> God's Word: *"For I know the thoughts and plans that I have for you, says the Lord, thoughts and plans for welfare and peace and not for evil, to give you hope in your final outcome."*
> -Jeremiah 29:11 AMP

When I arrived back to Indiana from our Christmas vacation, I started making the arrangements needed to move to Florida by August 1, 2001. I had to submit my resignation after teaching 20 years in the East Chicago school system and had to request recommendations, along with all the other requirements, to secure the new teaching job in Sarasota. I also had to start making arrangements to sell my property. Furthermore, that same semester, I had to start completing my loan application to purchase the Sarasota home from my parents. A lot was going on, but I was excited!

Everything was working out well, and I was on track to move down to Florida the last week of July. All of a sudden, I got a call from my mom during my family's 4th of July celebration down in Sarasota. She frantically told me that my dad had started having chest pains, and they had to take him by ambulance to the emergency room. She also informed me that they found out that my father needed to have open heart surgery immediately. What a shock! My heart sunk! "How could it be? Nooooooo! I was finally moving down, and my dad's health was at risk?"

Even though my official move was planned for the end of July, I instantly decided to fly down to be there for my father's surgery. When I got there, I was able to spend some quality time with him and kept taking pictures because it was such a delicate and special time for us. It was also special to be with my brothers and sister.

The open heart surgery went well, and afterwards my dad was his friendly, loving, and funny self. While still in the hospital recuperating, the siblings would take turns spending the night at the hospital with him.

On the third day after his surgery, it was decided that I would be staying to accompany him in the hospital room overnight. The family went home for the evening. He was okay for a while but was struggling trying to fall asleep. Then he started to complain that he couldn't breathe well. I told the nurse, but she said his vitals looked fine.

I tried talking with him, but it still looked like he was struggling, so I told the nurse again. I prayed with him and then decided to pick up a Bible to read him some encouraging words. Since he knew the Bible so well, I asked him what he would like for me to read, and he said **Psalm 23**. I started reading it in English, and he started reciting it by memory in Spanish. However, I noticed he was having an extremely hard time breathing and was barely able to speak, but he still ended the Psalm saying, "And I will dwell in the house of the Lord forever."

All of a sudden, he started losing consciousness and began to faint. I frantically ran out to the nurse's station and hysterically yelled, "He can't breathe, please help him!" Almost instantly about five people ran into the room with oxygen tanks to help him. At that moment, I felt like we were losing him. Without delay, I got on the phone and called my mom to tell her she needed to get to the hospital at once. She contacted my brothers and sister, and by 3 a.m., everyone was at the hospital.

By that point, they had taken my father upstairs to the intensive care unit. We were then allowed to go see him. When we saw him, he had a breathing tube down his throat, so he was unable to speak. I could tell he was surprised that we were all there.

All of a sudden, he opened his eyes very wide and was looking up. Then he started pointing at the hospital ceiling with his finger excitedly trying to ask us *something* ... We couldn't tell what he was trying to tell us since he had tubes down his throat, but were all anxiously trying to guess what he was trying to ask us.

At once, my brother, Danny, got a piece of paper and laid it on my father's stomach so he would write down what he was trying to ask us as he was laying down. He wrote something, but we couldn't tell what it was. Danny then gave him another piece of paper, and he again wrote the same thing, but we still couldn't read it. We were all frustrated but at the same time amazed that he was so energized and excited about whatever he was seeing. We kept trying to guess, but he would shake his head as he kept pointing to the hospital ceiling.

At that moment, a nurse walked in and said that my father was too agitated. She proceeded to inject him with something to calm him down and asked us to leave the room. Lamentably, when we came back in, he was asleep and never woke up for about two days. Then on July 12, 2001, he went to be with the Lord.

That was a painful tragedy and loss, which made us all extremely sad. A few days later, we had a very emotional funeral, which the whole family and numerous friends attended.

After the funeral, I had to go back to Indiana to finish my final preparations before I permanently moved back to Florida. It was devastating to think that I would finally be moving to Florida to live, but that my father was not going to be there, after all the years that he had been waiting for me to move down! That was an extremely emotional and sad time in my life.

One thing that was extra special to me, even to this day, that I got to share with everyone was that my father's last words were him speaking Psalm 23 while I was at his bedside at the hospital! That was so beautiful and symbolic to me—how my dad spoke God's words of inspiration and peace up until his very last breath.

> God's Word:
>
> "The Lord is my shepherd, I lack nothing.
>
> He makes me lie down in green pastures,
>
> He leads me beside quiet waters, He refreshes my soul.
>
> He guides me along the right paths for his name's sake.
>
> Even though I walk through the darkest valley, I will fear no evil, for you are with me, your rod and your staff, they comfort me.
>
> You prepare a table before me in the presence of my enemies. You anoint my head with oil, my cup overflows.
>
> Surely your goodness and love will follow me all the days of my life, and I will dwell in the house of the Lord forever."
> -Psalm 23 NIV

The other thing that was amazing is that a few months after the funeral, as my mom was staring out a window, it suddenly came to her what my father's final notes said. She deciphered that the words were, "Where is the hospital ceiling?" Apparently he was already seeing the heavens and the Glory of the Lord! No wonder my mother said that she had never, in their almost 50 years of marriage, seen that expression on his face! All this was an extraordinary experience that I will never forget!

My Father's Legacy

> God's Word: "What you heard from me, keep as the pattern of sound teaching, with faith and love in Christ Jesus. Guard the good deposit that was entrusted to you, guard it with the help of the Holy Spirit who lives in us." -2 Timothy 1:13

Since I was a little girl, I had always looked up to my father as a fun-loving, peaceful, and kind man. He had a passion for God's Word and loved to speak and preach in a very powerful way. Even after he retired and had moved to Sarasota, he had wanted to start a Spanish Ministry at the English church where he and my mother attended. After many years of trying, everything was finally approved. Even though he was 79 years old, his dream of starting a Spanish ministry as a side ministry of the English church finally happened in April 2001!

He knew that I had been involved in learning and teaching God's Word in Indiana and that I also played the guitar. That's why he was looking forward to me moving down to Sarasota so I could be involved in helping him with his new Spanish Ministry. Unfortunately, the desire of me joining him and participating in that ministry didn't become a reality due to his passing away only three months after he had finally started his dream Spanish Ministry.

Even though my father passed away, the Spanish Ministry continued with the guidance of a previous pastoral student of my father's when he taught at the Seminary of Puerto Rico. My brother Danny and I led the worship, the new pastor preached, and the ministry continued even though my father was not there. However, the ministry was not the same without my father being there, but we made the best of it. After a few years, I started going to a different English-speaking Church, but the Spanish Ministry at my dad's church continued.

The Spanish Ministry stayed alive and thriving for fourteen years, but by 2015, the ministry had not grown, and the English church couldn't afford a part-time Spanish pastor. They lost their pastor and ended up having someone from the church share a Bible message every Sunday. However, that person could only preach for three Sundays each month, and they needed someone to preach the last Sunday of each month.

One day I got a call from someone in the church. To my surprise, they asked me if I would be interested in teaching God's Word the last Sunday of each month. I was extremely humbled and honored to have the privilege of being asked to share God's Word at the pulpit of the Spanish Ministry that my father had started.

For a year I continued preaching God's Word on the fourth Sunday of every month until the main church's pastors decided that they were going to put an end to the Spanish Ministry because it was not growing. I was then told that the last Sunday would be December 27, 2015, which happened to be the last Sunday of the year. How incredible that fourteen years earlier my father had spoken the first words from that pulpit and that I would get to speak the last words from the *same* pulpit!

As I spoke on that last Sunday of 2015, with tears in my eyes, I boldly proclaimed at that pulpit that even though the Spanish Ministry was ending at *that* church, that nothing or no one would ever stop me from moving forward and speaking for God! My father's legacy, that *seed* he planted, actually lives within my heart forever, and I will continue to speak for God as long as I have life!

> God's Word: *"Being confident of this, that he who began a good work in you will carry it on to completion until the day of Christ Jesus." -Philippians 1:6*

Action—Chapter 8: A New Beginning

Applying God's Word: Ecclesiastes 3:1; Jeremiah 29:11; Psalm 23; 2 Timothy 1:13; Philippians 1:6

1. Have you ever wanted to have a new beginning or a fresh start in life? Please explain.
2. What has held you back?
3. Has there been a person in your life that has been an example or a mentor to encourage you? How?
4. What promise from God's Word can encourage you to move forward with your dreams?

Chapter 9

Defeating Unexpected Challenges

God's Word: *"Let us then approach God's throne of grace with confidence, so that we may receive mercy and find grace to help us in our time of need." -Hebrews 4:16*

I was finally living in sunny Sarasota, Florida enjoying my new life and the new home I had just bought from my parents. Even though my father had passed away the month before, my mom was relieved that I was now living in Sarasota.

Since the inside of my home was being totally remodeled, it worked out perfectly that I was able to live with her for about a month. During that month, I was able to help her with different things and get acclimated to living in Florida. It was a true blessing and emotionally healing for both of us to be together. I was also looking forward to the new school year so that I could start my new teaching job.

Before moving to Florida, I had been a third grade bilingual elementary school teacher in Indiana for about 20 years. I was honored to have been given outstanding recommendations from all my superiors. I had also been selected and included in "Who's Who Among America's Teachers" in 2000.

In addition, before I moved down, as the teaching arrangements were being finalized in Sarasota, three elementary school principals had requested that I teach in their school. It was up to me to make the decision. I chose to teach at Tuttle Elementary School because it had the highest Hispanic population. I felt that I could be of support for the students in that school and with the Hispanics in that community.

Even though I had requested the third grade level, I was assigned to first grade. My classroom also ended up being a portable classroom away from the main building. However, I didn't mind because I was just thankful I had a job and was now living in Florida and close to my family!

I decorated the classroom with the *smiley* theme and looked forward to meeting my students. I was not used to teaching the first grade level, but I did my best adjusting to the students' constant need for attention and guidance. Another challenge with my new teaching position was all the details, and the different educational techniques in that new teaching level, including the school system's rules, and procedures.

I felt that everything was going fine and I was adjusting well. The only thing was that after some classroom teaching evaluations, I was notified that I needed to attend additional training regarding the school system's teaching style. I didn't mind and looked forward to acquiring more knowledge so I could be a more effective teacher.

Nevertheless, one Wednesday afternoon in October, I received a letter asking me to attend a meeting at the principal's office. I didn't have the slightest idea what the meeting was going to be about. When I walked in, the principal and the vice principal were sitting side by side with a solemn look. I nervously sat down across from them wondering the purpose of my summons.

Then the main principal proceeded to tell me that since I was still on my 90-day probationary period, they were within their rights to let me go for any reason. They went on to say that they had decided that they did not want to keep me as a teacher and that I would have the option of either resigning or that I would be fired that Friday.

My heart sank! I was absolutely appalled! I couldn't believe what I was hearing! I sat there bewildered and confused, and immediately asked them "Why? What happened?" But they refused to explain, they just stared at me and shrugged their shoulders. I begged them, I kept asking them why, and all they said was to contact them in two weeks.

Why couldn't they tell me? What did I do wrong? I humbled myself and pleaded again, explaining that I had just bought a home and that I would do whatever they wanted me to do so I could keep the job. Again, they just sat there stone faced and unwilling to show any compassion, or to say anything.

At that moment, I felt helpless, frustrated, and hopeless! I didn't know what else to say. All I wanted to do was cry, but while sitting there motionless and numb, I closed my eyes and looked down devastated and in disbelief! Immediately my thoughts turned to God, and I realized that *He* was with me. I quietly prayed for strength and wisdom.

Then all of a sudden, I felt an overwhelming energy and fortitude. I looked up at both of them and boldly confessed, "That's ok, God will help me through this!" They still sat there with nothing to say. I then confidently got up, thanked them for the time I was able to teach there, and walked out believing in my heart that God would *really* help me.

I started thinking that even though that was such a tragic situation, I was thankful that I had gotten the job because it's what allowed me to be able to relocate to Florida and buy my home. Deep down I knew that God was with me and that He would make *a way* where there seemed to be *no way*. However, I still wondered what would happen next.

I decided to resign, due to "personal reasons," however I still could not believe what was happening. My whole life, and future, had been turned upside down! The main thought that kept overwhelming my mind was how was I going to pay for my mortgage payment for the house that I just bought and all my other living expenses if I didn't have a job?

The promise from God's Word that immediately surfaced in my mind, which encouraged me and gave me peace, was: *"But my God shall supply all your need according to his riches in Glory by Christ Jesus" (Philippians 4:19 KJV)*. It was like God was telling me all was going to be ok and that I just needed to continue to confess it, stay in action, and remain as positive as possible.

> God's Word: *"Therefore I tell you, do not worry about your life, what you will eat or drink; or about your body, what you will wear. Is not life more than food, and the body more*

than clothes? Look at the birds of the air; they do not sow or reap or store away in barns, and yet your heavenly Father feeds them. Are you not much more valuable than they? Can anyone of you by worrying add a single hour to your life?" -Matthew 6:25–27 NIV

I then realized that I had just sold my town house in Northwest Indiana and had some extra money in the bank. I was going to use it to pay off some credit card debt, but fortunately I had not paid it yet. I immediately decided that I would use that money to hold me over until I would figure out what to do for income. That sure was a blessing in disguise! God had prepared an *emergency savings* account, which I didn't even realize I was going to need until that moment.

Coincidentally (which I prefer to call a "divine coordination"), my sister Mimi was in the process of starting a new mortgage company in Sarasota. When she found out that I had lost my teaching job, she immediately said that she would train me so that I could work with her! What a godsend!

However, the main obstacle that I was concerned about was that I didn't know *anything* about mortgages. I was so ignorant about that field that a "good faith estimate" was like reading a foreign language to me. Mimi encouraged me and said I would do great and be able to replace my teaching income easily. At that moment, I was determined to do whatever it took to get educated in the mortgage field and to be successful!

Little by little, day by day, I would faithfully go to the office. I'd get on the phone, calling from lists that she would purchase, to find people who wanted to refinance their home or do a line of credit. It was definitely a steep learning curve, but with God's help, and asking a lot of questions, I knew that I would be able to do what needed to be done! Meanwhile, since the job at the mortgage company was not producing any income yet, I had to figure out a way to make extra income so my savings wouldn't run out. What would I do?

<u>God's Word</u>: *"Commit to the Lord whatever you do, and he will establish your plans."* -Proverbs 16:3

As I was driving to work one morning, I was listening to a Christian radio station that I loved because it was uplifting and positive. All of a sudden, a thought came to my mind, "Wouldn't it be great if there was a Spanish Christian radio station with uplifting music like this?" I thought about this because I was thinking of ideas *outside the box* to represent and work for God. That was truly my heart's desire.

One evening, I decided to attend a public event that the radio station was sponsoring. I wanted to personally meet some of the radio station DJs and ask them about any Spanish Christian stations in the area.

As I was talking to a DJ, a gentleman who overheard our conversation came to me and politely interrupted. He asked me if I knew of anyone who might be interested in working at the Living Word Christian Store in the Spanish book section. I immediately jumped at the opportunity and said that I was available and would be willing to work! We agreed to meet at the store the next day.

When I got to the store, I applied for the job, he asked me a few questions, and he hired me on the spot! He then told me he was the owner of the store and said he had been praying about finding someone to help Spanish speaking people in his store. It sure was an unexpected blessing, not only to get a job, but to be able to work with and for other believers!

The store even worked around my mortgage job schedule so that I could still continue working with my sister. It sure was a busy time working day and night, but with God's help I made it work. I continued working at both jobs and also started studying diligently to get my mortgage broker license. I eventually took and passed the Florida Mortgage Broker Exam and became officially licenced. God was definitely taking care of me!

My life was so different now! It had completely changed from being a licensed elementary school teacher, to my new career of now being a licensed Florida mortgage broker. In addition, as part of my mortgage job, I was also very involved with the Sarasota Chamber of Commerce activities and attended weekly realtor meetings and other community events for the mortgage business' marketing purposes. I eventually had to let go of the Christian store job, but it was definitely a wonderful privilege and experience.

> God's Word: *"Let your light shine before others, that they may see your good deeds and glorify your Father in heaven."*
> -Matthew 5:16

One day in 2004, as I was working at my mortgage office, I got a call from the editor of a newspaper stating that he had heard about me. He asked if I would be interested in writing a bilingual page for his monthly Christian newspaper, *The Lighthouse News*. I had never heard about it, but it was an English language local newspaper.

The man proceeded to tell me his desire was to reach the Spanish community, so he wanted to start a page called "El Faro" (meaning "Lighthouse" in Spanish). He was looking for someone to write a Biblical teaching in Spanish on one column and translate it to English right next to it. It was a volunteer opportunity, but it sure sounded interesting to me. I asked him who had told him about me, but he said he didn't remember. He had just heard that I would be excellent (God was working on my behalf!).

I accepted the voluntary position, and for two years, I wrote bilingual monthly articles in *The Lighthouse News* to spread the good news of God's Word! Some of the titles of the articles were "The New Birth," "The Renewed Mind," "Rejoicing in the Lord," "The Power of the Resurrection," and "The Inner Peace of God," just to name a few.

The commitment was a lot of work, but as I prepared, researched, translated, and typed the articles, it was a tremendous educational and empowering experience! I fell more and more in love with God's Word, and it was a true blessing to reach all kinds of people that I had never met with God's Word through that newspaper.

One day I received an email from a lady who had read my articles. She wrote:

"Dear Ruth, We subscribe to The Lighthouse News, and I have been using your articles to minister to the prisoners at the jail where my

husband and I hold services each Sunday morning. The pod of female prisoners that I work in has about five Hispanics along with the 25 English-speaking inmates, so I teach from your bilingual article, going back and forth between the English and the Spanish. It's the best material of its kind that I've come across!"

I was humbled by her email. She was asking for more of the articles so she would be able to continue teaching from them. I made sure she got all of them. It sure was a privilege to be used by God to be a blessing!

I never really knew how many people my "El Faro" Bible teachings reached or who was reading them, but I felt in my heart they were God's messages going out to people and that His Word does not return void! As it declares in *Isaiah 55:11, "So is my word that goes out from my mouth: It will not return to me empty, but will accomplish what I desire and achieve the purpose for which I sent it."*

That period of my life was definitely a time to hold on tightly to God's promises throughout all the challenges that I was facing—from losing my teaching job, to getting a miracle Christian store job, becoming a licensed mortgage broker, and getting to publish my own bilingual column in a Christian newspaper! It was amazing to see God's favor as He continued to *open doors* in very unique and unexpected ways!

Action—Chapter 9: Defeating Unexpected Challenges

Applying God's Word: Hebrews 4:16, Philippians 4:19; Matthew 6:25–27; Proverbs 16:3; Matthew 5:16; Isaiah 55:11

1. Have you ever had an extremely unexpected turn of events to your original plans?
2. What is the best way to try to handle a situation like that?
3. What can happen when we give God our concerns and continue to trust Him?
4. What has God promised about His Word when we share it and confess it?

Chapter 10

Transforming Your Life

God's Word: *"Let us not become weary in doing good, for at the proper time we will reap a harvest if we do not give up."*
-Galatians 6:9

My new life continued in Florida working as a mortgage broker with my sister Mimi. During that time, I met a lady who shared with me about a special program that was being offered at the Women's Resource Center (WRC) in Sarasota called Challenge. This was a three-week intense program for women who were going through transitions in their life and would teach them how to confront the challenges successfully.

Since I had been involved with the Hispanic Women's Forum in Northwest Indiana, I was very interested in finding out more about the newfound center. All the services they had available to help women were very impressive. Therefore, I decided to sign up and participate in the three-week Challenge Program. Some of the topics discussed were about changes in life such as self-esteem, goals, communication, relationships, abuse, finances, employment, health, and many more.

Throughout my life, even though with God's help I had made the best that I could during the difficult times, and felt I was doing okay, I was eager to learn more by participating in the program. I felt that it would be good to face my fears and challenges so that I could improve, let go of past hurts that I couldn't change, and feel more confident about myself.

God's Word: *"Be kind and compassionate one to another, forgiving each other, just as in Christ God forgave you."*
-Ephesians 4:32

One of the most damaging things that happened in my life that I had struggled with was when I was sexually molested by my grandfather when I was young. That experience had affected my self-esteem and had caused me to have many hidden fears and insecurities. To this day, I still cannot remember many experiences in my childhood.

I had also just gone through not only a first divorce, after 20 years of marriage, but a second divorce only after a one-year marriage. All this had totally shaken my world with frustrations, insecurities, and new challenges. However, learning to forgive was a key in helping me *let go*, and *let God*, so I could move forward in life.

As a grown woman, I had gone to therapists to help me deal with some of my issues. Thankfully, I always felt that no matter what I had gone through, God was still with me, loving me, protecting me, and guiding me. It was a constant battle in my mind, but by continuing to study God's Word, I had been able to overcome many of my mental challenges.

I realized that one of the ways I would cope with those issues was by staying busy with my family, my job, and being involved in many community activities helping people. I also avoided focusing on myself, and instead I constantly focused on God and His promises. God's Word in my life helped me have balance and stay sane!

In addition, I learned specific steps to learn to leave my past behind. First by acknowledging that terrible and unacceptable things had happened to me—and that none of it was my fault. Secondly, by realizing there was nothing I could do to change the past at *this* time. Thirdly, by forgiving others, and myself, so that I wouldn't live my life carrying all the guilt and condemnation in my mind. And lastly, by accepting God's pure, unconditional, and eternal love for me!

> God's Word: *"Who shall separate us from the love of Christ? Shall trouble or hardship or persecution or famine or nakedness or danger or sword? ... For I am convinced that neither death nor life, neither angels nor demons, neither the present nor the future, nor any powers, neither height nor depth, nor anything else in all creation, will be able to separate us from the love of God that is in Christ Jesus our Lord."*
> -Romans 8:35, 38–39

I sat through the Challenge Program being impressed with all the enlightening and informative material that was being presented. About halfway through the program, one evening I sat there pondering. Then all of a sudden, out of nowhere, I just happened to ask, "Do you have this class in Spanish?" The facilitator excitedly looked at me and said, "No, but would you like to start it and teach it?" At that moment, I was shocked and said no, being thunderstruck at her question. I thought "Who, Little ole me?" thinking it would be an extremely challenging endeavor to accomplish.

Even though I said I was not interested, the facilitator still decided to share my comment with the director of the center. I believe she saw some potential in me, that I didn't even see. A few days later, the director contacted me to have a conversation about possibly starting the course in Spanish.

Even though I thought it would be a terrific program for Hispanic women, I felt that it would be an overwhelming task to translate the whole three week program. I proceeded to tell her that I would do it but that we would need to put together a committee of people to help translate the hundreds of pages worth of material that was shared in the class to Spanish. She agreed and was committed to making it happen!

Within a year, a team of about five of us completed translating all the material. We decided to name the class "Retos" ("Challenge"). Then we proceeded to start advertising it to Hispanic women, organizations, and businesses in the area. I had the privilege of being the facilitator for the class. When we started it, we had about 15 women in the class. It was like a dream come true!

I definitely enjoyed the conversations and transformations that were occurring in the class. The symbol that I chose to represent the class was a butterfly. I gravitated to that symbol because they are so beautiful and free, but more importantly because the butterfly has always had a Biblical significance for me.

> God's Word: *"Be not conformed to this world, but be ye transformed by the renewing of your mind, that ye may prove what is that good, and acceptable, and perfect will of God."*
> -Romans 12:2 KJV

The word "transform" in Greek is "metamorphoo," referring to metamorphosis, the change that the butterfly goes through when it goes from a caterpillar to a beautiful butterfly.

As I facilitated the Retos classes, I literally had the privilege of seeing women's facial expressions, personalities, and ways of communication being transformed as they learned the class material. I could see that they were empowered and full of hope and had a new determination to face the world or whatever challenges they were going through.

It was also very special to know that even though all the women spoke Spanish, they represented various Hispanic countries and cultures! We had participants from Colombia, Cuba, Ecuador, Mexico, Panama, Peru, Venezuela, Puerto Rico, and others. It was so beautiful to be all together sharing, learning, and building an *international sisterhood*!

I remember that an older lady walked in to one of the classes with her granddaughter because she was insecure and afraid. She didn't even drive a car either. Well, by the time the program was over, she was confident, more joyful, and was determined to learn how to drive ... and she did! We also had a lady that didn't have a job and ended up starting her own dream Hispanic restaurant business! The benefits of that program were absolutely amazing!

Personally, this program proved to me the importance and power that our thoughts have. The ladies were *renewing* their minds and being transformed from "caterpillars to butterflies," and that was even without actually teaching the powerful promises from God's Word directly. I did, however, take whatever opportunities I had to share many of my personal testimonies of God working in my life, which were inspirational to all.

The word spread throughout the Spanish community about the work we were doing at the WRC. One evening, at an event I attended, I was approached by a magazine writer who wanted to talk with me about the Retos Program and how it was making a difference in Hispanic women's lives.

He was so impressed with what I had shared with him that he decided to write an article and entitled it "Women Helping

Women with Life Challenges (en Espanol)." It was published in the magazine *Sarasota Downtown and Beyond* in January 2008.

The article was a wonderful summary of the work we were doing and the positive changes women had achieved by participating in the program. I thank God that he opened the doors and gave me the courage to have started this marvelous life-changing Retos Program for Hispanic women in Spanish!

Even though I thoroughly enjoyed and loved to see the transformations that were going on with the Retos Program, I was a little disappointed that I was not allowed to teach anything directly from the Word of God. Sometimes I would share examples of what God had done in my life but was limited due to the rules of the center. I felt within myself that if I would've been able to include the Bible as a teaching tool, it would have taken the transformation to a new level with the promises and power of God's Word.

In the same year that I had started the Retos Program, God put a very special lady in my class and in my life. Liliana was an outgoing, positive, and extremely friendly Hispanic woman from Venezuela. She treasured the program so much that she kept participating in it. Since she seemed to be so interested, God prompted me to ask her if she would like to be trained to facilitate the class. She was very excited and immediately accepted. I trained her as she started assisting me with the class.

After that first year, she became the new Retos Program facilitator so I could continue to work on other personal projects. However, Liliana and I continued to work together organizing monthly "Open Houses" to keep promoting the program to Hispanics. My involvement and work with the WRC was definitely a great experience, but God was preparing me, as He had other "transformational" plans for my life.

God's Word: *"Your Word is a lamp to my feet, and a light to my path." -Psalm 119:105*

During that time in 2005, one of my daughters, Cristina, had come to live with me in Sarasota. She liked to watch a preacher lady on her computer with her headset on so I was unable to hear what the lady was saying. I would watch the lady walking back and forth on the stage waving her arms and being very dramatic while she was talking. I tapped my daughter on the shoulder and asked her who the lady was, and she said "Joyce Meyer."

Cristina shared with me that Joyce was a very *down to earth* and funny preacher, but that she taught a lot of God's Word in a real practical way. I had never heard of her, but I found out she was on TV, and I also started to watch her program daily. Everything she was saying made total sense, and I was learning lots of things that I could apply to my everyday life.

As I watched Joyce Meyer daily, it reminded me of the Bible teachings that I had learned about when I was in college in my early years. It was so heartwarming to be listening and learning from Joyce! She was definitely inspiring and always kept teaching and focusing on the power of God's Word. I also loved that the theme verse of her ministry is John 10:10, and the title of her TV program is "Enjoying Everyday Life."

> God's Word: *"I came that they may have and enjoy life, and have it in abundance (to the full, till it overflows)."*
> -John 10:10 AMP

I was excited about the new person I was becoming, like the transformation a caterpillar goes through to become a butterfly! I was definitely ready to refocus and recommit my life to God and to trust Him completely for whatever new plans He had for me to enjoy my everyday life!

Action—Chapter 10: Transforming Your Life

Applying God's Word: Galatians 6:9; Ephesians 4:32; Romans 8:35, 38–39; Romans 12:2; Psalm 119:105; John 10:10

1. What situations or experiences in your life have made you feel stuck or have held you back?
2. Is there someone, or even yourself, that you need to forgive to be able to move on? How will you do that?
3. How does realizing and believing that *nothing* will separate you from God's love impact your life?
4. What would life be like for you if you would transform some of your thoughts and start believing and speaking God's Word?
5. Where does *transformation* begin, and what steps do we need to take to start changing?

Chapter 11

Putting My Love Life in God's Hands

God's Word: *"But seek first his kingdom and his righteousness, and all these things will be given to you as well."*
-Matthew 6:33 NIV

I felt that I was living a really good life spiritually and materially. After all, I had my home in Florida, my dream convertible car, and God was providing for my financial needs. By this time, I was also Florida Notary Public, not only for the mortgage business I was in, but I had also been able to officiate a few weddings. God had also opened the doors for me to write bilingual Bible teachings in *The Lighthouse News* Christian newspaper, and in addition, He had helped me to start the Retos Spanish program at the Women's Resource Center. But most importantly, I was enjoying everyday life with amazing and practical Bible teachings from Joyce Meyer.

I had a lot to be thankful for, however, in my heart I was longing to be able to have a loving, faithful, and trustworthy companion. After my two divorces, I kept asking myself "What am I doing wrong? Will I ever find someone?" And at the same time I would tell myself, "You're better alone than with the wrong person." So I decided to focus on keeping God first in my life, and as I did, I knew that He would take care of the rest.

One day, as I was walking around in a mall, I made a decision to buy myself a ruby and diamond ring, to represent that Jesus was my *main love*. I wanted to put it on the finger where I used to wear my wedding ring. That ring became very meaningful to me because it reminded me about the *Virtuous Woman* described in *Proverbs 31:10–31* and how special I was in God's sight.

<u>God's Word:</u> *"A capable, intelligent, and virtuous woman — who is he who can find her? She is far more precious than jewels and her value is far above rubies or pearls ... Charm and grace are deceptive, and beauty is vain (because it is not lasting), but a woman who reverently and worshipfully fears the Lord, she shall be praised!" -Proverbs 31:10, 31 AMP*

One Saturday morning in August 2004, as I was browsing through my computer, an advertisement came up announcing a website called eHarmony for people who were looking for a companion. I had never seen anything like that before. I became intrigued and read all about the information and how it worked.

One of the aspects about it that interested me was that it was founded by Dr. Neil Clark Warren, a Christian theologian and clinical psychologist. He had made formulas, and algorithms, to be able to match people according to who they really were, from the "inside out." I browsed through the descriptions of several individuals, but there were no pictures and no way to communicate with anyone unless, of course, I signed up for their service.

I wasn't interested in signing up, that was until I saw on the top right corner of the website a little banner that said, "Try a one-week free trial." I thought about it for a moment and decided to sign up for the free week. However, I noticed that the trick was that you had to pay for a whole month, and if you cancelled within one week, you would get your money back. I told myself, "Ok, I'll try it," but I was determined to quit within the seven-day free trial period as I wasn't planning on being serious about finding a long-term relationship online and was only curious.

I then proceeded to answer about a 100 question detailed assessment. It was very enlightening, and I learned more about myself. I was also asked to complete two lists regarding what I "Must Have" and "Can't Stand" in a relationship. I was glad they had that, because I was planning to be very picky and not just let *anyone* into my life. Everything was completed, and I was ready to quickly start discovering my matches.

I officially started looking on a Sunday. I started my search near my city of Sarasota, and only got three matches, so then on Monday, I selected a 60-mile radius. Still the matches were very low, so I selected the whole state of Florida on Tuesday but saw no one of interest to me.

Since this felt like a game, I was just going to be on the site for only a week. Then on Wednesday August 11, 2004 at night, I decided to select the whole United States to see if there would be any matches. I was thinking that if there was a match out there anywhere under the *starry sky*, it sure would be interesting to find out!

On Thursday morning, when I checked, I was shocked to see all of the matches that were interested in communicating with me. However, I noticed one that stood out because he wanted a "Fast Track," which meant he wanted to go directly to emailing, which was very unusual, because everyone is supposed to go through the three stages of "communication" before the open emailing stage. I immediately declined the "Fast Track," wondering what the hurry was. My main goal throughout this search was to keep God first and have peace about this whole "match-making" process.

Even though I rejected the man's intent to "fast track" me, he still came back and asked me the five initial multiple choice questions. This made more sense to me, so I went ahead and answered his questions, and asked him five questions as well.

Amazingly we went back and forth through the other stages fairly quickly. By the way he answered his questions, he seemed very adventurous and thoughtful, and had a good sense of humor. His name was Dale Brewer. The funniest and most bizarre thing to me was that he was from Oregon—all the way across the whole United States!

It was now Friday, the sixth day of my free trial, and I was planning to stop the membership and close my account. That meant that I would be cut off from any method of communication with anyone, but I didn't mind. I had enjoyed my adventure with the website, and it had been interesting meeting and communicating with Dale. It was also a good day to quit because Hurricane Charlie was going to be hitting our area the next day, and I had to prepare my home before I left to shelter at my sister's house.

Even though Dale lived all the way in Corvallis, Oregon, and I wasn't sure if I'd ever meet him, he sure seemed like he could be a fun and interesting long-distance friend. So before I closed my account, on my answer to the last open-ended question, I told Dale that it was great meeting him, but that I was going to cancel. I also told him if he still wanted to communicate with me, I was including my private email. I said goodbye, closed the account, and continued my preparations before Hurricane Charlie landed.

When the storm had passed, and I ended up being able to log back into my computer, I was shocked that I had an email from Dale! We continued communicating directly through our personal emails, and our friendship continued to grow.

I remained strong and focused with my faith, my values, and what I was looking for in a friendship. We continued emailing for a few weeks and kept learning about each other. Finally, after a month, I decided that I was ready to start speaking on the phone and shared phone numbers. We ended up getting along so well that calling each other became a daily activity.

We were very compatible, enjoyed our conversations, and got along very well. Since we usually would speak at the end of the evening, one of my favorite things we did before we hung up is that we read a chapter from the Word of God and prayed. We started with the book of Proverbs and really connected, keeping God in the center of our long-distance friendship. It was very interesting that when God connected us, Dale was actually reading a book called *The Christ Centered Marriage: Discovering and Enjoying Your Freedom in Christ Together*.

During one of our conversations, I shared with him that it seemed that our relationship was growing, and I wished he lived closer. I proceeded to ask him, "With you living all the way in Oregon, and me in Florida, how would this relationship work?" I will never forget what he so confidently and peacefully said, "If God wants us together, He will work it out." Wow, his answer was brilliant! Why didn't I think about that? I absolutely loved his trust in God, and that if it was from Him, the relationship would work out!

> God's Word: *"But they that wait upon the Lord shall renew their strength; they shall mount up with wings as eagles; they shall run, and not be weary; and they shall walk, and not faint."* -Isaiah 40:31 KJV

After three months, we finally met in person when he flew to Florida to visit his parents' home, which *happened to be* only about an hour from my house! When I saw him in person for the first time, I felt like I really knew him. It was surreal, and we got along very well, like long-time friends! We decided we wanted to continue to see each other, so we took turns flying between Florida and Oregon (a seven-hour airplane ride) every 60 days.

We had so many adventures together in both locations: sightseeing, concerts, camping, watching football, cookouts, fishing, and many more. He actually taught me how to catch my first fish in the Willamette River in Oregon, which was an unforgettably exciting experience! I also truly enjoyed the get-togethers he would have in his home, and meeting all his wonderful family and friends! He sure had a lot of them, and they were all fun, kind, and loving … even to this day!

Our relationship continued to grow closer. After about six months, in February 2005, while Dale was visiting me in Florida, he took me to dinner on the 8th floor of the Lido Beach Resort. After an elegant meal overlooking the Sarasota Skyline, the waiter brought a beautiful dessert to our table. I looked at the waiter to say "no thank you," when all of a sudden I did a double take as I noticed there was a sparkling beautiful marquise diamond ring on top of the dessert! I was stunned! Immediately Dale asked me if I would marry him. I instantly said YES!

We agreed that we would live in Sarasota, so he would be relocating from Oregon. However, he told me that he needed to stay in Oregon for three more years until his son Jordan finished high school. That seemed like it was going to be forever, but I decided to trust God to make it work if it was *His Will*.

Our long-distance relationship continued strong for three years! I truly believe that having God in the center of our relationship is what kept it alive and growing. Dale ended up quitting his supervisor job, sold all his furniture, his beautiful home, and his truck. Then he gave his car to his son as a high school graduation gift. After getting rid of most of his belongings, he shipped a 4 x 6 POD box with what he wanted to keep. He was ready for a new beginning with me in Florida. God's plan was really working!

He moved to Florida at the beginning of June 2007, and we were finally married at Island Park by the Dolphin Fountain at Marina Jack in Sarasota, Florida on Saturday, June, 23, 2007. It was like a dream come true! Some of his friends came from Oregon, and his other family came from California and Canada, as well as my five grown children, my family, and my dear Sarasota friends.

What a glorious day and celebration! The best part was that Dale and I were finally companions together forever! We were committed to abide by what God's Word said about love so that we could continue to build our relationship with His loving guidance and wisdom.

> God's Word: *"Love is patient, love is kind. It does not envy, it does not boast, it is not proud. It does not dishonor others, it is not self-seeking, it is not easily angered, it keeps no record of wrongs. Love does not delight in evil but rejoices with the truth. It always protects, always trusts, always hopes, always perseveres." -1 Corinthians 13:4–7 NIV*

Now that we were together, we settled in our home. It was time to rebuild our new life together as husband and wife. For work, my sister Mimi welcomed Dale to join us to work at her mortgage company and kindly committed to train him.

Within a few months, he passed the state test and became a Licensed Florida Mortgage Broker. During that time, unfortunately, the housing crisis of 2008 started happening. I stuck around to help out with whatever loans I could do at the mortgage company, but Dale decided to look for a steady job.

As he went out looking for another opportunity to make money, he put his trust in God and had a great attitude and determination. Almost immediately, he found a job assisting a fishing boat captain. Shortly after that, he got his Florida Captain's License.

While working at the marina, God opened another door of opportunity; he was offered a full-time job as Facilities Manager at Marina Jacks and worked there for five years. Later he was able to get a job working at the School Board of Sarasota and has currently been promoted to "Lead Man" in the Facilities Department. He's always been a diligent, dependable, and excellent worker!

Since God was such a vital part of our relationship, one of our favorite things to do together was to attend church. We were looking for a way that we could get more involved, so we signed up to get training to be marriage mentors. We thought this would be a good fit, because we both had been married a few times. After all, we felt that we had learned a few things that we could share to help and encourage others to make their marriage and relationship work better.

In the program, we were assigned to have mentoring classes held in our home for married or engaged couples for 10 weeks. In the two years we were able to participate in the program, we mentored about five couples. The program proved to be an enriching and beneficial Christian program for the couples. It was also a wonderful way for us to strengthen our own marriage as we were helping others.

Through this experience of learning more about the beauty and blessing of marriage, I became more confident to officiate weddings as a Florida Public Notary. I would officiate beach wedding ceremonies and even had the privilege of marrying two of the couples we mentored.

At one time, I even considered starting my own wedding officiant business, but it just never worked out. It seemed like I enjoyed officiating, but mainly just for people I knew or by "word of mouth."

> God's Word: "...Though one may be overpowered, two can defend themselves. A cord of three strands is not quickly broken."
> -Ecclesiastes 4:9–12

Dale has truly been a wonderful husband too, exceedingly above what I even expected or imagined. He's always been adventurous, humorous, caring, and a fun-loving companion. He's a gentleman and has always treated me like his princess!

He also loves and lives by what he calls his 5 Fs: faith, family, fishing, football, and friends! He loves to bring me fresh flowers and surprises. He cooks, is very neat and organized, and is a talented handyman! He's also an excellent father to his only son, Jordan, and has also been very encouraging and supportive to my five children and three grandchildren. He has truly been a wonderful gift from God!

After having met Dale online within one week, during my free trial week, dating long distance for three years across the country, going through all our financial challenges, and having now been married for almost 14 years, people might wonder how we made it work.

First of all, no marriage is perfect. However, the key for us has been that we have always kept God first in our relationship. We read a daily devotional, pray, go to church together, trust each other, and try our best communicating, being patient, and having respect for each other. God's Word also has many promises to help make our life and marriage successful. As we learn them and apply them, we will continue to receive God's best for our life and our relationships.

> God's Word: *"Delight yourself also in the Lord and He will give you the desires and secret petitions of your heart. Commit your way to the Lord, (roll and repose each care of your load on Him); trust (lean on, rely on, and be confident) also in Him and He will bring it to pass."* -Psalm 37:4–5 AMP

Action—Chapter 11: Putting My Love Life in God's Hands

Applying God's Word: Matthew 6:33; Proverbs 31:10, 30; Isaiah 40:31; 1 Corinthians 13:4–7; Ecclesiastes 4:9-12; Psalm 37:4–5

1. Why is it so important to always keep God first in all we do?
2. How much do you value yourself? Do you see yourself as God sees you? If not, what should you do?
3. Have you ever made a list of "Must Have" and "Can't Stand" in a relationship? Why don't you try it?
4. What are some of the qualities of love expressed in 1 Corinthians 13?
5. What is the benefit of waiting on God and His timing?

CHAPTER 12

Handling Unexpected Disappointments

> God's Word: *"God is our refuge and strength, an ever-present help in trouble. Therefore we will not fear, though the earth give way and the mountains fall into the heart of the sea, though its waters roar and foam and the mountains quake with their surging." ... "Be still, and know that I am God; I will be exalted among the nations, I will be exalted in the earth."*
> -Psalm 46:1–3, 10 NIV

Have you ever felt like everything was stable and moving forward in a very good way, but all of a sudden you "hit a wall?" It's just like what we've been experiencing with the COVID-19 pandemic, which started in March 2020. Our whole world has been impacted emotionally, financially, and physically. It has been devastating to millions!

Something similar also happened to many people during the "Mortgage and Housing Crisis," which started in 2007. I had been trained and working as a Licensed Florida Mortgage Broker since 2001. I had finally learned so much about the mortgage business that I was confident and flowing with my knowledge, actively helping people from completing their mortgage loan application, resolving credit report issues, going through loan processing, all the way to the closing of the loans. I was really enjoying the opportunity of being involved in realtor and chamber of commerce meetings, and also marketing for our mortgage company.

However, in September of 2008, there was a significant disruption in the flow of loans and the collapse of the "housing bubble." Our mortgage loan business started to come to a halt. Mimi and I continued to work the mortgage business, but it became extremely difficult to keep the business going. Business was so slow that I would show up at the office and work all month, but not close any loans, which resulted in no income. Meanwhile, I was living off my credit cards, since I didn't have any cash flow, which also ended up creating other debt problems.

Ultimately by August 2009, Mimi decided she had to close the business, and that meant that I would have to find something else to do so that I could start having a positive cash flow. Honestly, I had been a little resistant about having to go work for somebody, because I had enjoyed seven years of being self-employed. However, due to the lack of income, the fact that I had drained my savings account, and that I had maxed my credit cards, I had no other choice.

> God's Word: *"Behold, I am doing a new thing! Now it springs forth, do you not perceive and know it, and will you not give heed to it? I will even make a way in the wilderness and rivers in the desert." -Isaiah 43:19 AMP*

I intensely started praying for God to lead me and to open doors of opportunity for something to show up so that I could start making money. I clearly remember there was a week in September 2009 that I was diligently determined to find a job, because I was headed to deep financial distress. I became desperate! Every day that week, I was relentlessly searching for jobs on the Internet and submitting my resume. I was truly doing my best, confessing God's Word, and completely trusting God to do the rest!

> God's Word: **"***This is the confidence we have in approaching God; that if we ask anything according to his will, he hears us. And if we know that he hears us, whatever we ask, we know that we have what we asked of him." -1 John 5:14–15 NIV*

Then on Friday, the last day of that week, about 5 p.m., a call came into my phone, but I was not able to get it. A man named John, a dean from Keiser University, left a message that he had reviewed an old teaching position application that I had submitted the year before! He was calling to find out if I was interested and to offer me a position as an adjunct professor to start teaching in two weeks! Wow, what an incredible and unexpected blessing! It looked like God was opening doors and possibly providing some income!

John wanted me to teach a one-month class at the university to students that were studying to be elementary school teachers. What an amazing promotion, from being an elementary school teacher myself, and having been let go unjustly of my Sarasota teaching job, to now being asked to teach teachers! God sure knows how to promote and bless His children!

The position was offered, and obviously I gladly accepted it! I taught the monthly class, which started in October. Then John asked me if I would teach two more classes in November. I was absolutely thrilled, and accepted. However, as an adjunct professor, I found out that they didn't have any long-term full-time positions. So I went back to God, asking, trusting, and believing that another opportunity would open up.

> God's Word: *"My eyes wait for You (looking, watching, and expecting) and You give me food in due season. You open your hand and satisfy me with favor."* -Psalm 145: 15–16

At the end of October, after I had accepted and committed to teach the two classes at the university, I got another surprise. I received a call from an office manager at the Consumer Credit Counseling Services (CCCS) of Atlanta stating that they were looking for a counselor to work full-time in Sarasota for one year. I could hardly believe what I was hearing.

The job position the man was referring to was a job that my sister had told me about, and that I had applied for about six months prior. Furthermore, the last time I had checked about the job on their website, the job was not listed any longer. Wow, where did this come from?

The CCCS were desperate to fill the position and needed me to start in November, but since I had promised John at Keiser University that I would teach the two classes, out of integrity, I had to tell the CCCS office manager that unfortunately I would not be available for the job until December.

Apparently, I gained favor from him, because he shared that they were really interested in me. He told me that he would check with his superiors to see if they could move the position forward so that maybe I could start in December instead. I prayed to God and trusted that His will would be done. Within a few days, I got a call confirming that the start date could be November 30th, 2009! I was thrilled and overjoyed!

On November 29th, which happened to be my birthday, the CCCS flew me up to Atlanta for a two week training. I was required to study and pass eight different exams to become a HUD Certified Bilingual Counselor. My job would be to help people with financial, budget, and credit counseling, with the long-term goal being financial success. I was also looking forward to my own financial success!

Even though they had told me the job in Sarasota was only guaranteed for one year because it was a city grant, I didn't care. I was just glad I would finally have some steady income. I totally trusted that God would provide my next job, as He had so faithfully done. I thoroughly enjoyed encouraging and relieving people from their financial stresses and especially helping them save their homes from foreclosures!

When the year was coming to an end, I received a call that CCCS had decided to keep me as an employee. That sure was a blessing and an answer to prayer that God was providing again! Since then, the non-profit agency has been through a few mergers and name changes. There have also been four different times in which previous coworkers have been laid off, but the agency amazingly has always kept me.

All continued well and wonderful, until October 2017 when I got a call from a human resources supervisor on a Friday morning. He told me that I would be laid off in two weeks and that I could leave the office at noon that day. My time had come to be laid off ... I was shocked and devastated!!

In the middle of my distress, I realized that I had counseling appointments scheduled for that afternoon and other people to call the next month to check-in with them. I immediately thought to ask the supervisor, "Who's going to be calling my clients?" He told me someone else would and not to worry about it. At that moment, I also thanked him for allowing me the privilege of working with the agency and that I knew it wasn't him personally that was letting me go. I then confidently confessed, as I was holding back my tears of emotion, "I know that God will find somewhere else where I can make a positive difference." He wasn't sure about what to say, but wished me the best and thanked me for my service.

> God's Word: *"To humans belong the plans of the heart, but from the Lord comes the proper answer of the tongue."*
> -Proverbs 16:1 NIV

That weekend, I felt a little numb and in disbelief, but at the same time, I was excited about what plans God might have in store for me. I started brainstorming about ideas of potential businesses I could start or where else I could find a job. I was back to the *drawing board*. The whole time I was prayerfully asking God to give me His wisdom and guide me.

I went back to my work office on Monday, thinking I had only two more weeks before I would be laid off. Then on Wednesday, I surprisingly got a call from the same supervisor. He explained that after our conversation on Friday he couldn't stop thinking about the positive things that I had said and admitted that the agency needed more compassionate counselors like me. He went on to say that he spoke with management and wanted to ask me if I would please stay and continue working with the agency.

Unbelievable! I had mixed emotions because I was getting excited about other opportunities, but at the same time, I was very thankful and accepted his invitation to continue with the agency. It sure was a blessing to get a confirmation that God was not done with me helping others through that agency doing my financial and housing counseling. I reflected on what had just happened ... Was that an attitude and trust "test"? It looks like I might have passed it!

No matter what happens to us, we should always keep a good attitude and believe that God is always working on our behalf. He will never let us down, as we keep trusting and loving Him!

God's Word: *"... As the Scripture says, what eye has not seen and ear has not heard and has not entered into the heart of man, (all that) God has prepared (made and keeps ready) for those who love Him (who hold Him in affectionate reverence, promptly obeying Him and gratefully recognizing the benefits He has bestowed)." -1 Corinthians 2:9 AMP*

Action—Chapter 12: Handling Unexpected Disappointment

Applying God's Word: Psalm 46:1–3, 10; Isaiah 43:19; 1 John 5:14–15; Psalm 145:15–16; Proverbs 16:1; 1 Corinthians 2:9

1. How do you usually handle unexpected disappointments?
2. Do you trust God and go to Him in prayer knowing He hears you?
3. How important is our attitude and what we say when we're faced with disappointments?
4. Why is it important to believe God's promises when things seem hopeless?

CHAPTER 13

Finding My Purpose

<u>God's Word</u>: *"He has saved us and called us to a holy life, not because of anything we have done but because of his own purpose and grace. This grace was given us in Christ Jesus before the beginning of time." -2 Timothy 1:9 NIV*

Throughout my life, I've always had a passion for helping people and making a positive difference for God. However, sometimes, I've felt like a "chandelier" instead of a "laser beam" for God. Like being busy, but not real productive and focused.

I knew that God has been working in me throughout my life. I believe that when we go through all the experiences, challenges, and situations in life, it is God molding us, training us, and testing us for future assignments and opportunities to represent Him.

As an example, when Dale and I got married in 2007, since he doesn't speak Spanish, we decided to start attending an English-speaking church. We went there for three years, but I felt like I was just going through the motions of just walking into church, listening to the wonderful message, and walking out. I felt like I was just *existing* and not really living a life of purpose and of serving God and his people. I wanted to do more to make a difference for God's Kingdom.

Through a friend of mine, I found out about a ministry called the "Foundation of Faith, Family, and Friends" started by Don and Katie Fortune. They had a special training class to develop teachers for a book and program called "Discover Your God-Given Gifts." When I heard about that, I was very excited and signed up to take the class and became a Gifts Certified Teacher.

I learned all about the seven "manifestation gifts" that God created us with as taught by the foundation. They explained that using the giftings described in *Romans 12:6-8*, people can learn more about how God created them to be. The categories are Teacher, Administrator, Giver, Exhorter, Compassionate Person, Discerner, and Helper. Without even realizing it, these giftings mold our personalities and help us find our purpose in life and how we can serve God and others more effectively with joy.

> God' Word: *"We have different gifts, according to the grace given to each of us. If your gift is prophesying, then prophesy in accordance with your faith; if it is serving, then serve; If it is teaching, then teach: if it is to encourage, then give encouragement: if it is giving, then give generously; if it is to lead, do it diligently; if it is to show mercy, do it cheerfully."*
> -Romans 12:6–8

One of my favorite parts of the training was that people could take an assessment to identify their gifts. When I did, I discovered that my three top "God-Given Gifts" were exhortation, administration, and compassion. I was so excited, and ready to start using them and to get more involved in the church and helping others.

Since I felt there was a great need for believers to know more about and discover their God-given gifts, I volunteered to be involved with the foundation. They had lists of hundreds of churches in the area, and my goal was to ask them if we could provide the presentation to help their members find their God-given gifts and strengths and to discover their main purpose in life. The assessment would also help people identify the ideal jobs that would bring them joy, based on their gifting. Furthermore, they could be more involved in a church ministry.

To my surprise, out of all the churches we contacted, only one accepted to have us teach the PowerPoint presentation and provide the assessment. It was disappointing that more churches were not interested. I thought maybe it was because most churches have their own programs to help their members. I also even made the class available to the church we were attending, but they had too many other things going on and were not interested.

My desire to be more involved in helping people continued, and I was not finding any way to make a difference. So Dale and I started attending another church to find a way to get more involved. One Sunday, I completed an outreach card that they gave all the attendees so they would get more involved in the church. I explained that I was a Certified Gifts Teacher and that I wanted to help with the women's ministry, but no one ever contacted me about it.

Even after all my efforts to find a way to help people discover their God-given gifts and their purpose in life, the "doors" didn't open. It sure was disappointing, because the "Discover Your God-Given Gifts" program was very detailed, applicable, and enlightening. To this day, I feel in my heart that people have a desire to find out their purpose in life or why they are here on earth. I still believe the need is there, however, I will continue to trust God and know He will guide my steps.

> God's Word: *"A man's mind plans his way, but the Lord directs his steps and makes them sure." -Proverbs 16:9 AMP*

The women's ministry at the church we were attending held a monthly program that I enjoyed attending in which they had a speaker and a potluck. A few hundred women from different area churches participated. I wanted to get more involved in helping, so I asked at one of the events what I needed to do to help as a "table captain," which was like the *host* of one of the tables at the event. I never got any responses. So I just continued attending the pleasant, delicious, and educational event.

Even though I was staying busy helping others and felt that God was with me, my search still continued to find a way I could share God's Word and encourage others with His Word. I was believing that *windows of opportunities* would open up for me to serve God more. Especially after the amazing miracle of God healing me after the brain tumor surgery in 2012. I prayerfully remained vigilant, looking for events and possibilities to get involved, meet people, and inspire others with God's Word.

> God's Word: *"I will instruct you and teach you in the way you should go; I will counsel you with my loving eye on you." -Psalm 32:8 NIV*

In the spring of 2014, my daughter Cristina invited me to attend a "God Encounter" weekend at her church in Orlando, FL. While attending that event, I felt an inner move from God that it would be fantastic to have an event like that at the women's ministry of the church I was attending.

When I got back to Sarasota, I immediately emailed the leader of our women's ministry, Tara. I wanted to share with her about the weekend and that God had put some ideas in my heart that I wanted to share with her. I also personally expressed to her that I wanted to be more involved in helping with the ministry.

Apparently it was a super busy time for her, because it took her 10 days to respond. When she finally replied, all she said was to please contact the lady in charge of "hospitality" so that I could be a greeter at the monthly events. I did, and served as a greeter, but I never got the opportunity to personally speak with Tara.

My search to be involved in the church and to work for God continued. At one of the events I attended, I found out about a one-day class called "Intimacy with Jesus" led and taught by a lady in our church named Connie. It sounded fascinating, so I decided to sign up and participate. (www.connielifevision.com)

At the class, we were asked to introduce ourselves in front of the group and to share something very intimate about why we were there. The leader wanted us to express our true desire about having a closer relationship with Jesus, and how we would *see* ourselves serving God.

I clearly remember that I excitedly and boldly shared, "I want to speak for God" (I had never verbally expressed it in that way). I loved the class, especially because the theme verse was *Romans 12:2* (the butterfly verse), which refers to transformation through the renewing of our mind to prove God's good, acceptable, and perfect will for us. After that class, I was never the same. I felt that God was very close to making something extra special happen in my life.

A few months later, on Saturday morning July 26, 2014, during my devotional and quiet time, God led me to a passage in the Bible. When I started to read it, I felt that it was God Himself commissioning me to speak for HIM. I got chills, felt emotional, and started to cry! This was God's message to me from His Word:

> *"Give thanks to the Lord, call on His name; make known His doings among the peoples! Sing to Him, sing praises to Him, meditate on, and talk of all His wondrous works, and devoutly praise them!*
>
> *Glory in His holy name, let the hearts of those rejoice, who seek the Lord!*
>
> *Seek the Lord, and His strength; yearn for, and seek His face and to be in His presence continually!*
>
> *(Earnestly) remember the marvelous deeds which He has done, His miracles, and the judgements He uttered."*
> *-1 Chronicles 16:8–12 AMP*

That was the beginning of a life changing and powerful week. The next day, on Sunday, the message from the pastor at our church was the Bible story of the sick woman who believed that if she touched the hem of Jesus' garment, she would be made whole *(Matthew 9:20-22 NIV)*.

It was powerful to hear Jesus acknowledge the woman by telling her, *"Your faith has healed you."* During the pastor's teaching of the message, God revealed to me that I had what it took to speak for Him. All I needed to do was to step out in faith, to be fearless about searching every opportunity, and to listen to Him, as He would direct my path.

> <u>God's Word</u>: *"Trust in the Lord with all thine heart and lean not unto thine own understanding, in all thy ways acknowledge Him and He shall direct thy paths." -Proverbs 3:5–6 KJV*

That Sunday night, I had a dream about sharing the testimony of the brain tumor from a podium in front of a large group of people. It was very inspiring, and people were commenting how they needed to hear that message.

When I got up the very next morning, since the dream was fresh in my mind, I started writing all the details of what had happened and everything that I could think of which was important to share. I kept thanking God for healing me, for His guidance, and giving Him all the glory!

Then on Tuesday morning, as I was reading a newsletter from the church, there was a section about the women's ministry, and it said to call or text Tara, the leader, to share with her what God was doing in our life to reach the women in Sarasota. I felt like that message was for me and that God was encouraging me to text her, even though I had not gotten much of a response from her when I had emailed her three months previously.

After debating in my mind, I decided to text her and told her that God had touched my heart in a big way and that I wanted to speak with her personally. To my surprise, she responded almost immediately and was available to speak with me that Thursday! I invited her to my home and told her I would make a special Puerto Rican lunch.

Thursday came, and there she was in my home! I was very excited to be able to share with her that I was ready to get more involved in the church and to find ways to be able to speak for God. I also mentioned to her that I would love to share my brain tumor healing testimony at one of the monthly women's ministry meetings.

Since she really didn't know me, I had prepared a folder with my resume and a list of the "El Faro" articles, which I had written for the Christian newspaper, and I included a sample of the bilingual Bible teachings. I also added a copy of the story that had been written in the *Sarasota Downtown & Beyond* magazine about the work I had done with the Spanish women at the Women's Resource Center. I was hoping to join her team and to help her in whatever way I could to reach women for God!!

She was very impressed and glad that I wanted to help out. She told me she'd take the information and pray about how I would be able to help. Then she went on to share with me that she was thrilled that she had just been invited to attend a Spanish Women's Ministry Conference in New Jersey and that she was going to be the keynote speaker!

My heart jumped, and I immediately expressed to her how exciting that sounded and that I would love to be a part of a ministry like that! She told me that the conference was going to be coming up the weekend of October 25, 2014. I was very curious about how she got connected with them, but she didn't share any details with me and started talking about something else.

Before she left my home, I decided to show her my office where I had my personal and work desks. I also wanted to take the opportunity to share with her how much I enjoyed learning God's Word with Joyce Meyer's teachings.

Joyce was a well known energetic, humorous, and powerful Bible teacher. By that time, I had attended about five different live Joyce Meyer conferences since 2005, watched her on TV daily, and also had a large collection of her books and CD's with teachings, which I would've loved to share with other women someday.

As we were standing in my office, all of a sudden God prompted me to ask her if it would be possible for me to coordinate and invite some of the women from the church and the women's ministry to attend a live Joyce Meyer Conference that was going to be taking place the weekend of October 23–25, 2014, in Tampa, Florida.

She briefly thought about it and said "sure." I asked her for any tips or suggestions since I hadn't quite organized an event like that, which would include carpooling and staying overnight at a hotel. Right away, she suggested that I should make the decisions that would be appropriate and whomever was interested and agreed would join me. I felt a little overwhelmed, but I was determined to do my best with God's help!

I was overjoyed that I would get to make available this amazing and free Joyce Meyer Conference to other ladies from our church. It was going to be a great opportunity to get to meet more church ladies and to be used by God to connect others to learning His powerful Word at the conference! I finally felt like I was fulfilling part of my purpose!

A few months later, Tara was looking for someone to assist the leader of the "table captains" at the Women's Ministry events, and my friend Connie, recommended me to Tara, because she had seen my organizational skills *in action* while working on coordinating the group that I was going to take to the Joyce

Meyer Ministries' Conference in Tampa. Tara then invited me to attend a leader's meeting. At the meeting, I suggested many ideas to improve the effectiveness of the "table captain's" roles and events. Because of that, she invited me to be part of her leadership group. Interestingly, I ended up leading a "table captain" training even though I had never had the opportunity to be a "table captain" myself. God sure is Awesome!

> God's Word: *"Commit your way to the Lord (roll and repose each care of your load on Him); trust (lean on, rely on, lien on and be confident) also in Him and He will bring it to pass."*
> -Psalm 37:5 AMP

Action—Chapter 13: Finding Your Purpose

Applying God's Word: 2 Timothy 1:9; Romans 12:6–8; Proverbs 16:9; Psalm 32:8; Romans 12:2; 1 Chronicles 16:8–12; Matthew 9:20-22; Proverbs 3:5–6; Psalm 27:5

1. Do you want to know more about your purpose in life? How can you find out?
2. Can you list some of the skills and talents you feel and believe you have (or that other people have mentioned that you're good at)?
3. In what ways do you think you can be used by God? How can you represent Him best in this world?
4. What action can you take today to start using your talents for God's glory?

CHAPTER 14

Divine Connections

> God's Word: *"Trust, (lean on, rely on, and be confident) in the Lord and do good; so shall you dwell in the land and feed surely on His faithfulness, and truly you shall be fed. Delight yourself also in the Lord, and He will give you the desires and secret petitions of your heart." -Psalm 37:3–4*

It was October 23, 2014, the time for the Joyce Meyer Conference in Tampa, Florida. A group of 25 women from our church had signed up to attend. The preparations, lists, and plans were ready. It sure had been a lot of work, with phone calls, coordinating rides, conference schedules, hotel rooms, and matching ladies so they could share a room, among other responsibilities. But I was thankful that God had given me the wisdom and favor to coordinate this first conference, I was thrilled!

As we had been making final arrangements for the three day conference, I had told the ladies that we would do our best to reserve seats together so that we could get to know each other. Even though most of the ladies that joined us went to the same church, most of them had never met each other, so it was a great opportunity to make friends and grow in the Word together.

Since I had already been to about five conferences, I shared tips with them and mentioned to them that if anyone wanted to see Joyce up close, we could make it happen. The plan was that when the worship time was going to start, we could get out of our seats, walk down to the front, and stand in front of the stage during the worship time while the band played.

At the end of the worship, Joyce would always walk to the front of the stage, greet everyone, and say a word of prayer.

I asked the ladies who wanted to participate, and about half of them decided to go down by the stage with me. It was a glorious time of praise and worship together!

The worship, presentation, and Joyce's teaching were very inspirational! In addition, since a lot of the women had only seen Joyce on TV and not in person, getting to see Joyce was extra special. The whole weekend was a huge blessing! We all came back to Sarasota *transformed* with a clearer understanding of God's love for us and committed to building a closer relationship with Him.

As I was reflecting, I remembered that I used to go to many of these conferences but with only one or two other people. At one time, no one was available to join me to go to Orlando to one of the conferences. I remember standing outside by my garden, not wanting to go by myself, and asking God, "Where are all the people in Sarasota that like to listen to Joyce Meyer that might enjoy going with me?" I was yearning to be able to meet people and have friends who loved God and enjoyed learning His Word.

I also had actually dreamed about starting a monthly Bible Study group. So as I had been working on coordinating the Tampa conference, I felt in my spirit that God was telling me, "This is your group that you yearned for, keep meeting with them." I immediately looked at my calendar, picked the third Monday of November, and told myself that I would invite all 25 ladies to my house for an "after the conference" get-together.

Also to continue the friendship, I invited the ladies to attend our next women's ministry event at the church, which was going to be the first Monday of November. I suggested that we could sit together and that I could reserve some seats. The ones who could attend happily agreed. I was delighted that we had a plan to continue to build our "sisterhood"!

The Monday of the women's ministry church event arrived. One of the ladies that had attended the Joyce Meyer conference was also a "table captain," so she reserved the seats at her table so we could all sit together. I was also excited about that evening because Tara, the leader, was going to be sharing about the Spanish Women's Conference that she had told me about and had spoken at in New Jersey in October. I had been very curious and wanted to hear all about it.

The event room had about 25 round tables, with seating for about 200 women. The evening program started, and we still had a few empty seats at our table. Out of nowhere, a lady, whom I had never seen before, approached me and asked me if she could sit beside me. I immediately said, "Of course!" We introduced ourselves. Her name was Iris (just like my mother's name), and she was very sweet and friendly. I asked her if she had been there before, and she said she attended the church and that she'd been to this event a few times, but didn't go all the time. We connected right away.

I asked if there were any groups she was involved with at the church. She shared with me that she was from the Dominican Republic and that she had just started a Spanish phone ministry with some ladies in New Jersey. She added that they had just finished their first conference in October. I immediately asked, "Was that the conference that Tara had just spoken at in New Jersey?" She cheerfully said, "Yes!"

I couldn't believe what I was hearing and seeing! God had placed Iris beside me and divinely connected us! He knew that deep down in my heart, I had wanted to know more about that Spanish Women's Ministry! I was astounded! What an unbelievable blessing to have the *actual person* who had started that ministry sitting right next to me!

I excitedly shared with her my desire to know more about her Spanish Ministry and that we definitely needed to talk! I immediately asked her why she was not sitting at the head table with Tara and the other dignitaries, but she humbly said, "I don't need to be there, especially since I'm so delighted to have just met you!"

About 10 minutes after we met, someone from the head table noticed Iris and came to escort her to the head table. We both smiled and pointed up to God! He must have been rejoicing that we both had finally connected! As Iris walked away, she told me to go to the head table to speak with her after the service and that she wanted to make sure that Tara knew that she had met me!

Afterwards, I walked over to the head table, and Iris told Tara, "I want you to meet my new friend Ruthie." Tara smiled and awkwardly said, "Yes, I know Ruthie. I'm glad you both met." That evening was a masterful God-ordained *Divine Connection*, which totally blessed my life! To this day, I'm still in awe of how God Works!

> <u>God's Word</u>: *"Now to Him Who, by (in consequence of), the (action of his power) that is at work within us, is able to (carry out His purpose and) do super- abundantly, far over and above all that we (dare) ask or think (infinitely beyond our highest prayers, desires, thoughts, hopes, or dreams.)"* -Ephesians 3:20

Within a few weeks, Iris and I, the "newly divinely connected friends," met for lunch to share with each other our goals and dreams to spread God's Good News. Even though she already had started a monthly phone ministry with two friends in New Jersey, Gricel and Teolinda, and I also had started my Joyce Meyer Bible Study Group, we both agreed that we wanted to work together for God.

We decided that in order to reach Hispanic women in Sarasota, we wanted to start an in-person monthly Spanish Bible study. We stayed in touch continuing to build our friendship and our goals for the Spanish group in our area. Meanwhile, God had other plans to prepare us by working together doing something else ...

> <u>God's Word</u>: *"(Not in your own strength), for it is God who is all the while effectually at work and you, (energizing and creating in you the power and desire), both to will and to work for His good pleasure and satisfaction and delight."* -Philippians 2:13

January 2015 started with two exciting Bible Studies for me to be involved with—the monthly Joyce Meyer Bible study home group and also participating in Iris' monthly phone ministry conference services. I was truly excited and thankful that I finally was reaching out and involved in making a positive difference to reach people for God!

During that same period of time is when I had been asked to preach at my father's Spanish Ministry once a month. Since my new friend Iris and her husband Tony spoke Spanish, they asked if they could go to be a part of the service. It was a great opportunity to continue building our friendship. So they, along with my husband Dale and my brother Danny, also attended and participated in the Spanish Ministry service each time I would preach.

To my surprise, I found out that Iris and Tony had been worship leaders in a previous church. Since the Spanish Ministry didn't have a formal worship team, they accepted my invitation to help me lead the worship. Iris had a beautiful and angelic voice, and Tony was an excellent and talented guitar player. I loved harmonizing with Iris and together we were all able to be inspired as we praised and worshipped God.

They were whole-heartedly committed to help with worship during those fourth Sundays of each month. That year as we worked in the church's Spanish Ministry together, it became a strong foundation for what God had planned for us. Even though it was sad to have seen the Spanish Ministry come to an end December of 2015, we were determined to keep God's Good News message alive!

At the start of the new year, January 2016, we decided to officially set a start date for our Sarasota Spanish Women's Bible study group, which Iris and I had spoken about and had been talking about since we had first met.

We decided to invite bilingual women from the Spanish Ministry Church we had attended and also reached out to some of the Hispanic women that I had met at the Women's Resource Center. We decided to meet at different ladies' homes, which we believed would create a friendly and inviting atmosphere and *sisterhood*.

We started the Spanish group in February 2016 and continued to meet monthly for over three years. Once a month, we connected over the phone with the group from New Jersey, and on a different day of the month, we met in person with the ladies that lived in Sarasota. Then every year, our goal was to do an annual in-person conference together with the ladies from New Jersey.

The Spanish Ministry continued, and the ladies became like a family. Lamentably, in the summer of 2019, our dear sister Iris got sick for about six months. She was in and out of several hospitals, and her health kept declining. Unfortunately, our beloved friend Iris passed away on January 18, 2020.

All of us were stunned and devastated! We could not understand why such an amazing, loving, and faithful friend who had definitely dedicated her life to God and had made such a huge difference in our lives had died prematurely.

It was extremely sorrowful and hard to comprehend, but that's when our faith in God's comfort and His peace held us up. We had hope, because we knew of the promise of eternal life and knew that we would see her again when Christ returns!

> God's Word: *"Brothers and sisters, we do not want you to be uninformed about those who sleep in death, so that you do not grieve like the rest of mankind who have no hope. For we believe that Jesus died and rose again, and so we believe that God will bring with Jesus those who have fallen asleep in him ... Therefore encourage one another with these words."*
> *-1 Thessalonians 4:13–18 NIV*

Iris left us a beautiful and powerful legacy, and we are committed to continue the Spanish Women's Ministry. Since I was a co-leader with her here in Sarasota and shared the same vision, the group has definitely continued under my leadership for God's glory!

I am extremely thankful that we have a team of four ladies in our leadership team: Elizabeth, Gloria, Karen, and Yolanda. We named the group "Nueva Vida" (New Life) to signify the new life and transformation we can go through as we renew our minds and believe God's Word. We also have a Facebook page to reach other Hispanic women who love God and who want to be stronger and learn more of His Word.

We meet monthly for a Spanish Bible teaching and sharing. We also started a new Bible study curriculum called "Nueva Vida en Cristo" ("New Life in Christ") to help us get more rooted in Christ. We'd love to meet in person, but due to the Covid-19 pandemic of 2020, we've had to meet on Zoom. Just recently however, God has *opened the doors* for us to meet at Grace Community Church as a "Grow Connect Group"! We are thankful that we will continue to have the privilege of reaching and teaching more people that want to learn God's message in Spanish!

I am in awe that God has allowed me to continue the legacies of my father's and Iris' Spanish Ministries here on earth while I have the privilege of still being alive, with the hope that one day we'll all be together again!

> God's Word: *"But as for you, continue in what you have learned and have become convinced of, because you know those from whom you learned it, and how from infancy you have known the Holy Scriptures, which are able to make you wise for salvation through faith in Christ Jesus."*
> -2 Timothy 3:14–15

Besides the work with the Spanish Women's Ministry, God has continued to grant me favor to continue leading the Joyce Meyer Bible study group. We had started meeting in November 2014 in my home with about 12 ladies. However, by the next summer, my living room was getting too crowded with about 20 ladies. I didn't know where we would meet, but I was trusting God that when we needed another place, He would provide it in His timing.

It just happened that the next month, Anne, a friend from church had started attending the Bible Study at my home. She shared with me that she had just moved to a place where they had a community center. She graciously made available for us to have the monthly studies there. The room was spacious, and was equipped with tables and chairs. It even had a kitchen area and a stage; and best of all, there was no fee to hold our meetings there. We were extremely thankful and blessed there!

To make the Bible studies more meaningful and educational, we decided to start studying Joyce Meyer's book, *The Battlefield of the Mind*. Every month we would watch a portion of Joyce's teaching on CD. We then would review and discuss a handout that I had prepared that would emphasize the teaching and Bible verses from the lesson. We've also been able to study several of Joyce Meyer's books including *Making Good Habits Breaking Bad Habits*, *Never Give UP*, and *The Mind Connection*.

In 2015, we started a Joyce Meyer Bible Study Facebook page to be able to stay connected with some of our friends that lived out of town. The Bible study on Facebook has continued to grow for the last six years, and we now have over 13,000 people that have asked to join from all over the world.

It's truly been an amazing blessing to see and hear how people are eager to learn more of God's Word and be able to apply and be blessed by the promises in His Word. Through our Facebook page, it's been a great way to stay connected by sharing positive messages and encouraging Bible scriptures. We also show our monthly Bible Study on Facebook LIVE so others that are outside of our Sarasota area and throughout the world can also join us.

Our Sarasota group has attended all of Joyce Meyer's Florida conferences since 2014. Then in October of 2018 we even organized a Live Stream of the Joyce Meyer's "Love Life" Women's Conference" at a church in town. We have been able to reach out and have touched many women's lives from various churches and walks of life with the powerful and encouraging message from God's Word.

For the last few years, God has also provided a fabulous team of five ladies (Karen B, Karen M, Bobbi, Cathy, and Cheri) to assist me every time we have a Bible study or any other activities. I am extremely thankful to God for their love, support, and their faithfulness!

Throughout the six years we've been having our monthly Bible study—since 2014—we've had some challenges of where to meet, but God has always provided a place. Dale and I started attending Grace Community Church in Sarasota, Florida, and they have graciously opened their doors for our group to meet at their location to study the Bible, thanks to our dear friend, Pastor Amy.

We've become one of the church's Connect Grow Groups, which we now call "Growing in Christ." We are still studying Joyce Meyer materials, but our main goal is to study God's Word and to grow in our knowledge of being more like Christ so that we can have more victory in our life.

Furthermore, as of March 2021, our Nueva Vida Spanish Bible study group has also been included as one of the Connect Grow Groups at Grace! I am definitely thankful and looking forward to growing our group in Spanish and reaching out to even more people in our communities to spread the Good News of God's Word!

Throughout my life's challenges, I have witnessed God's faithfulness! He continues, and will always continue, to work in our lives by granting us favor and opportunities to serve Him as His *ambassadors*. We must never quit or give up! Our part is to remain faithful to Him with a thankful attitude, to do our best, and also to be patient about His timing to work in our life.

> God's Word: *"And therefore the Lord (earnestly) waits (expecting, looking, and longing) to be gracious to you: and therefore He lifts Himself up, that He may have mercy on you and show loving-kindness to you. For the Lord is a God of justice. Blessed (happy, fortunate, to be envied) are all those who (earnestly) wait for Him, who expect and look and long for Him (for HIs victory, HIs favor, His love, His peace, His joy, and His matchless, unbroken companionship)!"*
> -Isaiah 30:18 AMP

Action—Chapter 14: Divine Connections

Applying God's Word: Psalm 37:3–4; Ephesians 3:20; Philippians 2:13; 1 Thessalonians 4:13–14; 2 Timothy 3:14–15; Isaiah 30:18

1. What heart desires or dreams do you have that will make your life more fulfilling?
2. Have you ever had any unexpected surprises from God? Please explain.
3. What is the hope we need to have when someone we love dies?
4. As you trust God and commit to Him whatever you do, what will happen?

CHAPTER 15

The Miracle of Transformation

God's Word: *"He gives strength to the weary and increases the power of the weak. Even youths grow tired and weary, and young men stumble and fall; but those who hope in the Lord will renew their strength. They will soar on wings like eagles; they will run and not grow weary, they will walk and not be faint." -Isaiah 40: 29–31 NIV*

I have realized that life is all about changes, transformations, and new beginnings. As believers in Christ, our ambition once we accept Christ as our savior,is to renew our mind so that we can learn the privileges and benefits of being a child of God.

We should transform from what the "world" teaches and expects to what God's Word teaches and promises! We must be committed to not only read His Word but also be ready to confess it boldly and REALLY trust God when challenges and storms come our way.

Challenges in life never stop! Again I was faced with another lay off. It happened right before Christmas of 2019. I was definitely shocked and concerned, but at the same time, almost automatically, I started to think about all the promises in God's Word that would encourage me to have hope. I didn't know what I would do, but with God's help, I was confident we would figure it out. I've come to realize that "believing" is like a *muscle*, the more we work it, the stronger we get and the faster we can overcome our challenges.

The New Year 2020 arrived and I was looking forward to what God had in store for me. I started communicating with my sister, Mimi, and thinking about ideas to maybe start a new business with me. Since we both were Licensed Florida Notary Publics, we decided to start a business to do mobile notary signings. We took further classes to be better prepared for the work ahead, created a website, and were in the process of making business cards and starting our marketing plan. We felt we would have good success with this kind of business.

Meanwhile, during this time, since I didn't have a full-time job, I was also able to meet one-on-one with each of the ladies in both the Spanish and English Bible study groups so I could get to know them even better. I was also able to devote more time to planning and studying the Bible study group materials. It was definitely a time to get reorganized, and refocused. I saw it as a new opportunity to continue to work for God wherever he needed me.

When March 2020 came, no one ever imagined the devastation that was going to change our country and our world ... the Coronavirus Pandemic! All our gatherings and activities came to a halt as we all had to stay indoors and avoid being in groups. A lot of changes started to take place. There were a lot of questions, confusion, and emotional distress.

When frustrations, depression, and tribulations start attacking our life, we must realize we are in a spiritual battle. It's a time to recognize that we have a God who ultimately has the master plan, and we must continue to proclaim and believe His promises!

> God's Word: *"Peace I leave with you: My (own) peace I now give and bequeath to you. Not as the world gives do I give to you. Do not let your hearts be troubled, neither let them be afraid. (Stop allowing yourselves to be agitated and disturbed; and do not permit yourselves to be fearful and intimidated and cowardly and unsettled.)"* -John 14:27 AMP

One day towards the end of March, my third month of not having a job, as I was sitting at my desk happily working on some projects, I got a text from the manager, Misty, of the job that had laid me off in December. She wanted to know if I had another job. I was taken aback by her question. I answered, "No, why?" She explained that she wanted to know if I was available to work with the agency again, because the phones were *ringing off the hook* and they needed more counselors.

What had happened was that due to Covid-19 and all the shutdowns that were going on, people were losing their jobs and therefore unable to afford their mortgage payments or their rent. I was totally taken off guard, as I was already getting used to my new life, but I gladly accepted to go back and was rehired on April 1, 2020 as a HUD Certified Bilingual Counselor.

God knew all along what the plan with my work would be. The way it worked out for me was that I got like a three month paid vacation (two months of severance pay and one month of unemployment benefits). I also got the opportunity to individually meet with my sisters in Christ, and I was also able to reorganize my office and make my room look like new again to be ready to serve God at a higher level.

What I have learned in life is to always do my best, have a good attitude while I'm going through challenges, and God will always do the rest, as I rest in Him ... *letting go* and *letting God*. He will find ways to communicate with us and to reveal Himself and His Will to us. While we go through stages and challenges in life, God finds ways to help us "see" and understand messages He has for us.

Some ways I have learned that God communicates with us are through His Written Word, the Bible; through His Spirit that lives in us; through nature, His creation; through prayer; through songs and music; through other believers and people; and through circumstances. His desire is for us to have an intimate relationship with Him and to be transformed from the inside out, to have freedom, and to live the more abundant life Christ came to make available!

> God's Word: *"Don't be conformed to this world, (fashioned after or adapted to its external, superficial customs) but be transformed (changed, Greek/ metamorphoo— like a butterfly's transformation) by the (entire) renewal of your mind (our ways of thinking, with new ideas, and new attitudes), so that you may prove what is the good and acceptable, and perfect will of God, even the thing which is good and acceptable and perfect in His sight for you!"* -Romans 12:2

I have loved butterflies, especially in the last 16 years of my life, and have always been in awe of the transformation that they go through. Isn't it mind-boggling that a caterpillar that is crawling on the ground is transformed into a beautiful butterfly that flies freely wherever it wants? And how about all the varieties and how colorful they are? They are a work of art by our Creator! Have you ever seen the cycle the caterpillar goes through to become a butterfly? It is a miraculous transformation!

Butterflies are so meaningful to me, because I feel God's love when I see them. I believe that God wanted to impress upon me His love by having me have an extraordinary and life-transforming experience with a real butterfly.

On the morning of July 16, 2020, I walked out to my garden and spotted a pupa hanging from a rod iron trellis (a pupa is the nonfeeding stage between the larva and adult, during which it undergoes a complete transformation within a protective cocoon or hardened case.) I was absolutely amazed that I could clearly see the wings of the butterfly inside. I immediately ran back into the house to get my camera, because I had never seen a real live pupa, much less with a butterfly inside like that.

When I came back, to my amazement, the butterfly was, at that very moment, coming out of the pupa! I couldn't believe my eyes! I immediately started videoing the miracle I was seeing as the butterfly's little sticky legs were trying to maneuver itself as it was dangling in mid air, until it was able to hold itself to the edge of the rod iron edge.

It was an absolute phenomenon! The whole process took only about five minutes! The timing of it all also blew my mind! How absolutely perfectly that God had placed me right there at that moment to see the butterfly coming out of the pupa to be set free! I was in total awe of God's creative power!

The very next weekend, I was taking my friend Karen to my garden area and was excitedly telling her about the miracle of the butterfly coming out of the pupa. All of a sudden, a butterfly that looked just like the one that I had seen come out of the pupa was gracefully flying around us.

Unexpectedly, it decided to land on my jeans below the left side of my knee. I was thrilled that a butterfly had landed on me, so I asked my friend to take a picture right away before it flew away. I was expecting the butterfly to fly away, but it didn't. It actually stayed right there by my knee. I walked in and out of the house and did whatever I needed to do, and the butterfly stayed on my leg. I was elated and absolutely blessed!

Since the butterfly wasn't moving or flying away, I kept staring at it up close to see if it was stuck or even still alive. After it being on my pant leg for about three hours, I was concerned that maybe something was wrong with it. I then decided to go outside and lift its little body with a piece of paper to see it was still alive. I also decided to take a video, to remember this spectacular event. As I lifted the butterfly from the bottom part of its body, it literally started walking up my knee to my thigh and kept walking up to my waist. It started walking faster, then it flew away!

Wow, what a beautiful experience! I kept wondering ... why did the butterfly stay on my pant leg for so long? Did it feel comfortable with the warmth of my jeans, or was God trying to send me a very special message through nature? It was a phenomenal experience! I really felt that God was right there speaking to me through that amazing live butterfly!

A few days later, as I again walked out to my garden to enjoy the flowers and God's beauty, I happened to see a caterpillar crawling on a milkweed leaf and was surprised. Then I saw another one, and another one, and another one ... the whole area was loaded with caterpillars! I counted 10 of them! They were absolutely perfect, a beautiful lime green with black lines separating the sections of the body.

I then decided to check out another area where I also have milkweed plants, and again, the area had another six caterpillars crawling around! So I saw a total of 16 caterpillars! I wondered what was happening. Did that mean I was going to have a *butterfly farm*? I was again so excited! I immediately started wondering about what God was trying to communicate to me through this third miracle regarding *transformation*.

I specifically started praying for Him to communicate the meaning of these three miracles: seeing the butterfly coming out of the pupa, the live butterfly being on my pant leg for three hours, and then seeing 16 bright and beautiful caterpillars crawling around in my garden. I felt that God was trying to tell me that it was *time* for me to come out of *my pupa*, and to start flying! I kept praying for His guidance.

Interestingly enough, a few days later, I got a call from a publisher. You see, God had put on my heart to write a book after the brain tumor surgery about seven years prior. I had felt that He wanted me to share my healing testimony and how His Word and confessing His promises had helped me heal. I believed in my heart that I should, and would, share this miracle, but I had kept putting it off not knowing how to go about writing the book, being insecure about the whole process, and not knowing where to start.

I had told my family and talked with the women in my Bible studies about wanting to write a book. I had attended free webinars to learn more about how to write a book, and I even contacted a few publishers. However, nothing had really materialized.

I kept projecting by when I would have the book done, but I kept moving the year. I finally decided the year 2020 would be a cool year to have a book written. It was already June of 2020 and time was running out, so when the publisher called this time, although I was busy, *something* made me take the call.

The publisher explained to me that they could publish my book but that I had to provide them with a manuscript. Well, the manuscript is what I actually needed help with, but all the lady said was that I'd have to look online to find help. She also said that once I gave them the manuscript, it would take at least six months more to publish it. The conversation was very informative, but I still felt perplexed on how to do the actual writing of the book. I asked God to please help me make a way, where there seemed to be no way, so that I could really have a book published before the year 2020 ended.

> God's Word: *"Jesus looked at them and said, 'With man this is impossible but with God all things are possible.'"*
> -Matthew 19:26 NIV

Exactly two days later as I was sitting at my desk at work, I looked down at my cell phone and noticed an announcement for a free webinar about "How to Write a Book in Less Than 3 Months"! What an unbelievable surprise! It was going to start in only three minutes! I briefly thought about it, for about one minute, and then immediately decided, "Why not? Let's find out how to get this book finally written!"

I watched the webinar, and it was very informative. I was very energized to find out more and finally have the guidance I need to write my book. The presenter, Chandler Bolt, also made available a free book called, *Published*, that he had written about how to publish a book, along with a free audiobook. I started reading it, and it all made a lot of sense. I was genuinely committed to get it done this time!

I decided to sign up right away to get the training and support of the Self-Publishing School at the end of June 2020. I was excited to be able to learn all the ins and outs of how to write a book. I participated in many coaching sessions and spent hours dedicated to the dream of finally writing my book come true by Christmas! However, since 2020 ended up being such a difficult year, and had so many negative memories for so many, it was suggested and I decided to have the book published in 2021.

I started 2021 with a new challenge *right out of the gate* ... Dale and I got infected with Covid-19! What a way to start the year! We immediately stopped working and started taking the precautionary steps to take care at home. We were extremely tired and had most of the regular Covid-19 symptoms, but thank God we didn't have to go to the hospital, and now we are healthy again. So I'm back to writing and finishing my book!

Somehow, I really believe the experiences with the three butterfly miracles were a way that God was preparing me to truly transform my thinking to get this book written. I was ready to share my passion, my testimonies of God's miracles in my life, and to encourage others to learn about the plan of salvation and eternal life!

I also wanted to share that people can transform their life by believing that God's Word works and by applying it to their life! What a blessing and a privilege it is to help others by sharing my own story of transformation!

> God's Word: *"Finally, be strong in the Lord and in his mighty power. Put on the full armor of God, so that you can take your stand against the devil's schemes. For our struggle is not against flesh and blood, but against the rulers, against the authorities, against the powers of this dark world and against the spiritual forces of evil in the Heavenly Realms. Therefore put on the full armor of God so that when the day of evil comes, you may be able to stand your ground, and after you have done everything to stand."* -Ephesians 6:10–13

As long as we're living in this world, we will always have all kinds of problems and challenges. We might not understand why bad or tragic things happen especially to believers or innocent people. However, remember that no matter what happens, God has promised us that something good will come out of it.

One of my favorite verses that has always kept me strong and trusting in God no matter what happens is *Romans 8:28 AMP*, *"We are assured and know that (God being a partner in their labor) all things work together and are (fitting into a plan) for good to and for those who love God and are called according to (His) design and purpose."*

When we believe God's Word, love Him with all our heart, and trust that He has a good plan for our life, we will have the courage to do our best and have God's peace as we trust that He will do the rest. We need to guard our heart and stay strong believing His Word and all His promises.

In conclusion, as I've been writing this book and looking at my life, I have truly realized that God was always at work within me. I feel that He was preparing me throughout my life as I was going through different challenges and experiences to be able to go through the devastating challenge of having major brain tumor surgery. Even though I was facing death, that is exactly when I REALLY started to live and appreciate God's master plan for my life!

I am thankful that God has healed me and has given me a chance to continue to live, for His purpose and for His Glory!

I will forever continue to make a positive difference for His Kingdom by sharing that His Word *really works* as we believe it and apply its principles in our life!

I trust that you have also been encouraged and inspired to believe His Word and to receive God's gift of eternal life through his son Jesus Christ who died to make it available for you because He loves you! Why not start, or continue, your mental transformation to live the more abundant life, which Jesus came to make available and which is possible to ALL who believe that His Word absolutely works!

> God's Word: *"And we also thank God continually because, when you received the Word of God, which you heard from us, you accepted it not as a human word, but as it actually is, the Word of God, which is indeed at work in you who believe."*
> *-1 Thessalonians 2:13 NIV*

Action—Chapter 15: The Miracle of Transformation

Applying God's Word: Isaiah 40:29–31; John 14;27; Romans 12:2; Matthew 19:26; Ephesians 6:10–13; Romans 8:28; I Thessalonians 2:13

1. Are you a "caterpillar," are you in a "pupa," or are you flying in life like a "butterfly" living a fulfilled life with purpose?
2. What will it take for you to become a *butterfly* and start *really living* your life?
3. Has God been "speaking" to you about something you should do but haven't done?
4. What physical or mental roadblocks are holding you back?
5. What promise from God's Word are you going to believe to encourage you?
6. What results and benefits will you experience as you achieve your transformation?

Acknowledgements

To God, I am eternally thankful to you for giving me earthly life, and eternal life, for healing me, and encouraging me to write this book about the power of your Word which has transformed my life and given me a purpose for living.

To my dear mother Iris Grace Gonzalez Ph.D., and my father Rev. Nicandro E. Gonzalez Ph.D. I am deeply thankful and blessed for your love, and for raising me in the ways of God, being excellent role models, and always wanting the best for me. I trust you are smiling at me from heaven.

To my husband, Dale Brewer, thank you for all your love, support, encouragement, and patience while in our journey through life, especially while I've been writing this book. You have brought joy and adventure to my life. I thank God for joining us as companions in life! I love you!

To my sister Mimi Gonzalez, thank you for your love, and for always being there for me during my many ups and downs in life, in sickness and in health, and everything else in between. Thanks for leading the way as you wrote your book *Always Wear Your Lipstick*, for the heartwarming and loving poem "Blue Moon Blessing", and for all the editing, words of wisdom and guidance as I worked on this book. (www.mimi-gonzalez.com)

To my daughter, Melisa McCann, thank you for praying for me, encouraging me, and for following in my footsteps with leading Bible studies, community events, and taking your musical talents to the next level. I was also blessed with the loving and inspiring prayers from my precious grandchildren Nick and Melodie (www.facebook.com/melisa.mccann.music).

To my daughter, Elena Uttaro, thank you for always being so caring, giving, and generous with our family and for always being so dependable. You are also an awesome and loving mom to our sweet granddaughter Emma, who is also my diligent and darling *Mariposa (Butterfly)* cookie assistant.

To my daughter, Selina Benavente, thank you for inspiring me to share my message and to encourage others in this world through social media! You have been a living example of making your traveling dreams a reality, and I am truly blessed that we've had such special times together!

To my daughter, Cristina Ally, thank you for telling me about Joyce Meyer, for your help with all your technological savvy, and for the photo shoot. You've been a great example of determination by starting your own counseling business, and I love your sweet and loving spirit. (www.flourishcounseling.co/)

To my son, Tony Benavente, thank you for loving and forgiving me, you are my only son, and nothing will ever separate me from loving you. I'll never forget how extra special it was when you showed up as "bee keeper" at my door to let me know you loved me! I love you TOO!!

To my friend Karen Barichak, thank you for your support, suggestions, and ideas as we have worked together in the Women's, English, and Spanish ministries, and especially for stepping in to help edit my book. I deeply appreciate you from the bottom of my heart.

To my precious sisters in Christ Bobbi Berhalter, Karen Makowski, Cathi LaRose, Cheryl Ison, Susan Burt, Karen Memory, and Juanita Flores. Thank you for all your words of wisdom, cheering me on, and believing in me as I was writing this book. Your support, leadership, and encouragement have kept our Bible studies vibrant and growing for God's glory!

To my beloved friend Iris Division, (and her supportive husband Tony), it was a true blessing joining forces with you as we started the Spanish Women's Ministry together in Sarasota. I loved how you endearingly called me "teacher", and kept encouraging me to write this book. I regret that I didn't write it while you were living, but you have definitely been with me in spirit. I love you, and you are forever in my heart. I'm looking forward to being with you again, in heaven.

To my Spanish Bible Study "Nueva Vida" and our faithful leaders Elizabeth Rodriguez, Yolanda Rios, Gloria Orjuela, Karen Barichak, and also Gricel Rodriguez, and Teolinda Acevedo, thank you for always being a strong foundation, so that we can continue learning God's Word together, and for being supportive every step of the way as we continue to grow in Christ.

To Amy Gaston, Pastor Chip Bennett, and Grace Community Church, thank you for always being so welcoming, supportive, and loving in allowing our Bible study groups to gather in your church. I truly appreciate being part of our church's mission "to be intentional neighbors that reflect Christ". (www.gracesarasota.com)

To my Christian author friends and mentors Bonnie Joy Kelly, *Morning Coffee*; Gail Sullivan, *The Red Shoe Project*; and Jane Blakewell, *Sink or Swim*, and *Angels in Disguise*. You have been an inspiration to me and amazing role models of God's faithfulness. I thank God for you.

Thank you also to Sky Rodio Nuttall for being one of my book editors, to the 100 Covers team for coming up with such an inspiring book cover, and to Joris Sharpe and Arjen Broeze at Cutting Edge Studio for coordinating and finalizing the ebook and paperback book formatting. Great teamwork!

I also want to thank Chandler Bolt and the Self-Publishing School (SPS) community for all the coaching, and support throughout my book writing process, and to the Facebook Mastermind Community for all their "likes", messages, and encouragement. It was amazing to be surrounded by such talent worldwide!

Last but not least, I want to acknowledge my launch team and YOU, for picking up this book and taking the time to read it. I trust that as you've enjoyed it and worked on the "Applying God's Word" sections. I hope that you have been encouraged, inspired, and transformed as you've learned God's Promises, and believe that God's Word Works!

"Blue Moon Blessing"
August 31, 2012

To you, Ruthie. My sister, my friend~

Once in a Blue Moon we find someone like you
Someone trusting and friendly so honest and true.
I've written this poem from my heart and my mind
To you, my dear sister, so loving and kind.

Tonight is your night, full of wonder and might.
This night of a Blue Moon floating plainly in sight.
It's a rare moment, a wonderful treat,
Two full moons in August, glowing brightly with heat.

And you're just like this Blue Moon, all that know you agree
You spread joy to those near you, always giving for free
Without judging or asking, always sharing your cheer
Those around you are blessed knowing that you are here.

This Blue Moon tonight is incredibly rare
Just like you, my dear sister, one who loves and who cares
Loving sister and friend, caring mother and child,
Faithful lover and wife, gentle spirit that's mild.

You're delightfully beautiful, all inside and out
Just look in the mirror, and you'll have no doubt.
Like the moon in the sky, you're a sight to behold.
You're more precious than diamonds and silver and gold.

This world is so blessed to have someone like you
Like the moons and their cycles, weather normal or blue
Please know we appreciate what you give to us all
Speaking words of encouragement in the moments we fall.

On this Blue Moon tonight we will make one more plea
To the God all around us, even though we don't see
We ask him to hold you and cure you throughout
And we're certain He listens, not a glimmer of doubt.

So onward we journey on this path we must take
Full of courage and peace knowing He won't forsake
On this beautiful Blue Moon, and event that is rare.
Just know you are special, and we love, and we care.

By: Mimi Gonzalez

Have you Received God's Free Gift of Salvation?

> God's Word says: *"For the wages of sin is death, but the gift of God is eternal life in Christ Jesus our Lord." - Romans 6:23*

God's gift of Salvation is free to us, but it cost God the life of His only Son Jesus. He paid for our salvation with His blood by dying on the cross. But then God raised him from the dead in victory! Now we can have a new life, and an intimate relationship with Him.

> *"For God so loved the world, that he gave his only begotten Son, that whosoever believeth in Him should not perish, but have everlasting life. For God sent not his son into the world to condemn the world; but that the world through him might be saved." - John 3:16-17*

Where will you meet your loved ones when you or they physically die? Do you have an "exit plan"? Accept God's free gift of eternal life and meet in heaven, by believing in Jesus who gave His life for us and has prepared a place for us in heaven!

> *"Jesus said to her, "I am the resurrection and the life. The one who believes in me will live, even though they die, and whosoever lives by believing in me will never die. Do you believe this?" - John 11:25-26*

Do you have to work to be *good enough* to earn God's gift of Salvation? NO!

> *"For by grace are ye saved through faith; and that not of yourselves: it is the gift of God: Not of works, lest any man should boast." Ephesians 2:8-9*

How do I accept God's free gift of Salvation? By believing His Word, through faith in Jesus!

> *"That if you confess with your mouth, "Jesus is Lord," and believe in your heart that God raised him from the dead, you will be saved. For it is with your heart that you believe and are justified, and it is with your mouth that you confess and are saved." Romans 10:9-10*

Prayer for Salvation

Dear Heavenly Father, Thank you for giving your son Jesus' life for me and for raising him from the dead. I confess Jesus as my Savior and Lord and invite Him into my heart and life. Thank you for forgiving my sins and for the gift of eternal life. I want to trust and follow You as my Lord and Savior, and to have a personal relationship with you! Amen.

Index

Promises from God's Word

Bible / God's Word 148	Love 152
Salvation / God's Gift 148	Mind 152
Children 148	Needs / Protection 152
Comfort 148	Patience / Waiting 153
Courage / Confidence 149	Peace 153
Death 149	Plans / Purpose 154
Discipline / Obedience 149	Power 154
Faith 149	Prayer 154
Favor 149	Rest / Stress 155
Fear 150	Speak / Words 155
Forgiveness / Guilt 150	Spiritual Warfare 155
Health 150	Temptations/Self-Control .. 156
Help 150	Thankfulness 156
Hope 151	Trouble / Trials / Worry 156
Joy 151	Trust 157
Life 151	Truth 157
Light 152	Wisdom 158

Bible / God's Word

Psalm 46:10
Joshua 1:8
John 1:1
2 Timothy 2:15
Psalm 18:30

Psalm 119:74
Matthew 4:4
1 Thessalonians 2:13
2 Timothy 3:15-16
Hebrews 4:12

Salvation / God's Gift

John 3:16-17
John 11:25-26
Acts 2:21
Acts 16:30-31
Romans 6:23
1 Corinthians 15:1-11
Ephesians 2:1-10
2 Timothy 3:14-15
1 Peter 1:23
1 John 4:9-10

John 10:9-10
John 14:6
Acts 4:12
Romans 5:6-21
Romans 10:9-10, 17
2 Corinthians 5:20-21
1 Timothy 2:3-4
Titus 3:3-8
1 John 2:1-2
1 John 5:11-12

Children

Psalm 34:11
Psalm 103:13
Proverbs 22:6
Proverbs 31:28
Ephesians 6:1-2
3 John 1:4

Psalm 78:6-7
Psalm 127:3-5
Proverbs 29:17
Matthew 19:14
1 John 3:2

Comfort

Psalm 31:7
Psalm 62:2
Matthew 5:4
2 Thessalonians 2:16-17

Psalm 34:18
Psalm 119:50
2 Corinthians 1:3-7

Courage / Confidence

Deuteronomy 31:6
Psalm 4:8
1 Corinthians 15:57-58
Hebrews 4:16

Joshua 1:9
Matthew 14:27
1 Corinthians 16:1
1 John 5:14-15

Death

John 11:25-26
Romans 6:3-11
1 Corinthians 15:51-57
Hebrews 2:14-15

Romans 5:10-17
1 Corinthians 15:20-26
1 Thessalonians 4:13-18

Discipline / Obedience

Jeremiah 7:23
Proverbs 8:35
Luke 11:28
1 Corinthians 15:58
Titus 1:8-9
Hebrews 12:1-11

Proverbs 3:11-12
Proverbs 19:20
John 14:15
2 Timothy 1:7
Titus 2:1-8
2 Peter 1:5-10

Faith

Matthew 9:20-22
Mark 11:23
Romans 10:17
Galatians 3:24-25
Hebrews 10:22-23
James 2:17-18

Matthew 17:20
Romans 5:2
2 Corinthians 5:7
Ephesians 3:12
Hebrews 11:1,3,6

Favor

Psalm 5:12
Psalm 69:13
Proverbs 3:3-4
Proverbs 12:2
James 4:6

Psalm 30:5,7
Psalm 84:11
Proverbs 8:34-35
2 Corinthians 6:2

Fear

Deuteronomy 31:6
Psalm 23:4
Psalm 91:4-5
Proverbs 3:24
Isaiah 35:4
Isaiah 41:10
Hebrews 13:5-6b
Joshua 1:9
Psalm 34:4
Psalm 112:7-8
Proverbs 29:25
Isaiah 54:14
2 Timothy 1:7
John 4:18

Forgiveness / Guilt

Psalm 34:18
Psalm 103:3,11-12
Romans 4:7-8
Romans 12:19-21
Philippians 3:12-13
Colossians 3:12-13
1 John 1:9
Psalm 86:5-7
Matthew 11:24-25
Romans 8:1
Ephesians 4:32
Colossians 2:13-15
James 5:15-16
1 John 2:12

Health

Psalm 30:2
Psalm 107:20
Psalm 147:3
Isaiah 58:8
Jeremiah 30:17
1 Peter 2:24
3 John 1:2
Psalm 103:2
Psalm 118:17
Proverbs 4:20-22
Jeremiah 17:14
Matthew 9:22
James 5:14-16

Help

Psalm 18:29-30
Psalm 55:22
Psalm 121:1
Isaiah 41:10,13
Isaiah 58:9a
Hebrews 13:5-6b
Psalm 28:7
Psalm 94:17-19
Psalm 145:18-19
Isaiah 50:7
Hebrews 4:16
1 John 5:14-15

Hope

Psalm 25:3-5, 21
Psalm 33:20-22
Psalm 147:11
Romans 8:24-25
Ephesians 1:18
Colossians 1:27
Hebrews 11;1
Psalm 31:23-24
Psalm 42:5
Proverbs: 23:18
Romans 15:13
Ephesians 4:4-5
1 Timothy 4:10
1 Peter 1:3,13,21

Joy

Nehemiah 8:10
Psalm 33:21
Psalm 89:15-16
Psalm 118:24
Proverbs 21:15
Isaiah 61:10
Habakkuk 3:18
Philippians 4:6,10-11
Hebrews 12:1-3
Psalm 5:11
Psalm 68:3
Psalm 100:1-2
Psalm 119:74
Isaiah 55:12
Jeremiah 15:16
John 15:11
1 Thessalonians 5:18
1 Peter 1:8

Life

Psalm 16:11
Psalm 121:5-8
John 3:16
John 10:10
Romans 6:4,8-10
2 Corinthians 5:17
Colossians 1:10
1 Thessalonians 4:7,11-12
2 Peter 1:3-4
Psalm 104:33
Proverbs 4:20-23
John 6:35
John 14:6
2 Corinthians 4:10-12
Galatians 2:20
Colossians 3:3-4
2 Timothy 1:9-10

Light

Genesis 1:3-5
Psalm 18:28
Psalm 119:105, 130
John 1:4-9
2 Corinthians 4:4-5
Colossians 1:12-14
1 Peter 2:9
Revelation 22:5

Psalm 27:1
Psalm 89:15
Matthew 5:16
John 12:46
Philippians 2:14-16
1 Thessalonians 5:5-6
1 John 1:7

Love

Psalm 13:5
Ecclesiastes 4:9-12
John 3:16
John 14:21
Romans 5:8
1 Corinthians 13:4-7
Ephesians 3:7-19
1 John 4:7-12

Proverbs 8:17
Mark 12:30-31
John 13:34-35
John 15:9-17
Romans 8:37-39
Ephesians 2:4-7
1 John 3:18

Mind

Isaiah 26:3
Romans 8:5-8
Romans 15:5
2 Corinthians 10:3-5
Ephesians 4:23-24
Philippians 4:6-9
1 Peter 1:13

Matthew 22:37-38
Romans 12:2
2 Corinthians 4:4
Ephesians 3:20
Philippians 2:1-5
Colossians 3:2
1 Peter 5:8-9

Needs / Protection

Deuteronomy 33:12, 27
Psalm 5:11-12
Psalm 91:1-16
Psalm 121:5-8

Job 11:18-19
Psalm 23:1-6
Psalm 112:7
Psalm 32:7-8

Proverbs 18:10
Matthew 6:25-34
John 17:11-15
Hebrews 6:18
1 Peter 3:13-14

Isaiah 43:1-2
Philippians 4:19
Hebrews 4:16
2 Thessalonians 3:3

Patience / Waiting

Ecclesiastes 3:1-8
Psalms 31:24
Psalms 40:1
Psalms 62:5
Isaiah 40:29-31
Romans 5:3,4
Galatians 6:9
Hebrews 6:11, 12
James 1:2-4,12
1 Peter 5:6

Psalms 27:14
Psalms 37:34,7
Psalms 42:5
Isaiah 30:18
Lamentations 3:24-26
1 Corinthians 2:9
Colossians 1:11, 12
Hebrews 10:23
James 5:7-8
Revelation 3:10

Peace

Psalm 4:8
Psalm 85:8
Proverbs 14:30
Isaiah 9:6-7
Isaiah 32:17-18
John 14:27
Romans 5:1
1 Corinthians 14:33
Ephesians 4:3
Colossians 3:15
Hebrews 12:14

Psalm 29:11
Proverbs 3:1, 17
Proverbs 17:1
Isaiah 26:3
Isaiah 54:10
John 16:33
Romans 8:6
Ephesians 2:13-18
Philippians 4:6-9
2 Thessalonians 3:16
James 3:18

Plans / Purpose

Esther 4:14
Psalm 33:11
Psalm 40:5
Proverbs 16:1-3, 9
Isaiah 43:19
Jeremiah 29:11
1 Corinthians 3:6-9
Philippians 1:6
2 Timothy 1:9-12

Psalm 20:4
Psalm 37:4-5
Proverbs 15:22
Proverbs 19:21
Isaiah 55:9
Romans 12:6-8
Ephesians 2:10
Philippians 2:12-16
1 Peter 4:10-11

Power

Psalm 46:10
Psalm 66:3-7
Proverbs 18:21
Jeremiah 32:17
Luke 10:19
Romans 1:16
1 Corinthians 1:17-18
Ephesians 1:17-23
Philippians 2:13
Philippians 4:13
2 Timothy 1:7

Psalm 62:11-12
Psalm 77:14
Isaiah 40:26, 29-31
Matthew 19:26
Acts 1:8
Romans 4:20-21
2 Corinthians 12:9-10
Ephesians 3:16-21
Philippians 3:10
Colossians 1:11

Prayer

Job 2:27
Psalm 17:60
Psalm 145:18-19
Isaiah 30:19
Jeremiah 33:3
Matthew 7:7-8,11
Matthew 18:19
Luke 18:1
John 15:7
Romans 12:12

Psalm 5:2-3
Psalm 91:15
Proverbs 15:29
Jeremiah 29:12
Matthew 6:5:15
Matthew 11:24
Matthew 21:22
John 14:1-14
John 16:23-24
Romans 8:26-27

Ephesians 1:16-17
Philippians 1:4-6
1 Thessalonians 5:16-18
James 5:13-16
1 John 14:1-14

Ephesians 6:18-20
Philippians 4:6-7
Hebrews 4:16
1 John 3:22

Rest / Stress
Psalm 16:9-11
Psalm 39:6-8
Psalm 91:1
Isaiah 40:29
Matthew 11:2-30
Hebrews 4:1-11

Psalm 37:5
Psalm 62:1-2,5-8
Psalm 127:2
Matthew 6:25-34
Philippians 4:6-9
1 Peter 5:7-11

Speak / Words
1 Chronicles 16:8-12
Psalm 34:12-13
Proverbs 13:3
Proverbs 16:23-24
Isaiah 50:4
Matthew 12:34-37
Ephesians 4:29
2 Timothy 4:2

Psalm 19:14
Proverbs 4:24
Proverbs 15:1
Proverbs 18:21
Isaiah 55:11
Acts 5:20
1 Thessalonians 5:17
1 Peter 3:10,15

Spiritual Warfare
Deuteronomy 28:7
Matthew 16:23
Acts 10:38
Romans 7:23-25
Romans 16:20
2 Corinthians 11:13-15
1 Timothy 6:12
1 Peter 5:8-9
1 John 3:7-9

Psalm 35:1-3
John 10:10
Acts 26:17
Romans 8:37-39
2 Corinthians 10:3-5
Ephesians 6:10-17
1 Peter 2:11, 12
1 John 4:4

Temptations / Self-Control

Proverbs 1:10,15
Matthew 6:13
Mark 1:12-13
Luke 22:40
1 Corinthians 10:13
1 Timothy 1:9-10
Titus 2:11-14
Hebrews 4:15-16
James 1:13-15
1 John 3:7-9

Proverbs 4:14-15
Matthew 26:41
Mark 14:38
Romans 12:21
Galatians 5:19-25
2 Timothy 1:7
Hebrews 2:17-18
James 1:2-3
James 4:7

Thankfulness

Psalm 7:17
Psalm 100:4
Psalm 118:19-21
Luke 22: 17-19
Romans 7:25
1 Corinthians 15:57
2 Corinthians 9:15
Philippians 1:3-4
Colossians 3:15-17
1 Thessalonians 5:18

Psalm 30:4
Psalm 107:1,8
Luke 9:16-17
Romans 6:17-18
1 Corinthians 14:16-19
2 Corinthians 2:14
Ephesians 5:20
Philippians 4:6-7
1 Thessalonians 2:13
Revelation 11:17

Trouble / Trials / Worry

Nahum 1:7
Psalm 27:5
Psalm 34:17-20
Psalm 50:14-15
Psalm 91:15
Psalm 138:3,7-8
Proverbs 11:8
Isaiah 58:9

Psalm 9:9
Psalm 32:7-8
Psalm 46:1-3
Psalm 86:6
Psalm 107:13-14
Psalm 143:10
Proverbs 15:15
Isaiah 61:3,7

Matthew 6:25-34
John 14:27
Romans 8:31-35
2 Corinthians 2:3-4
Philippians 4:6-7
James 1:2-4
1 Peter 3:14

John 16:33
Romans 8:28
2 Corinthians 1:4
2 Corinthians 4:8-9,17-18
2 Thessalonians 1:5-7
James 5:13
1 Peter 5:7

Trust

2 Samuel 22:31-33
Psalm 28:7
Psalm 37:3-5
Psalm 62:8
Psalm 125:1
Proverbs 3:5-6
Isaiah 30:15
Romans 15:13
1 Peter 5:7

Psalm 18:2-3
Psalm 31:14-15
Psalm 56:3-4
Psalm 84:11-12
Psalm 143:8
Proverbs 29:25
Jeremiah 17:7-8
Romans 8:28

Truth

Deuteronomy 4:29
Psalm 89:14
John 4:24
John 14:6
John 17:17
Ephesians 1:13
Ephesians 6:14
2 Timothy 2:15
2 John 1:1-4

Psalm 25:5
Matthew 5:6
John 8:32
John 15:25
John 18:37
Ephesians 4:15
1 Timothy 2:4-7
1 John 3:18-19
3 John 1:4

Wisdom

Psalm 111:10
Proverbs 2:1-6
Proverbs 3:13-18
Proverbs 9:10-12
Proverbs 19:8.11
Ecclesiastes 7:11-12
1 Corinthians 2:1-8, 13
James 1:5-8

Proverbs 1:7
Proverbs 3:5-7
Proverbs 4:5-11
Proverbs 16:16
Proverbs 24:14
1 Corinthians 1:18-25
Colossians 1:9-10
James 3:13-17

Resources

Hall, Emily. 2018. *What is the Bible and where did it come from?* https://www.crosswalk.com/faith/bible-study/what-is-the-bible-and-where-did-it-come-from.htm

Meyer, Joyce. (2020) *Do It Afraid* (1st Edition) New York, NY; FaithWords Hachette Book Group, Inc. www.joycemeyer.org

1988, May 5th. "School Suspends Teacher" *The Times Newspaper p.1 (front page) (Article about when Ruth was suspended)*

2005-2006 "El Faro" Bilingual Columnist Bible Teachings *The Lighthouse News; Sarasota, Florida*

2008, January. "Women Helping Women with Life Challenges (en Español)": *Sarasota Downtown and Beyond. (Article about Ruth's work at the Women's Resource Center; Sarasota, Florida.)*

Gonzalez, Mimi. (2019) *Always Wear Your Lipstick.* Sarasota, Florida:. (Ruth's sister's book that explains the tumor story in Chapter 3 "The Black Pearl").

Websites:

www.BibleGateway.com
Read/search words in many languages & versions

www.flourishcounseling.co
Counseling by Cristina Ally (Ruth's daughter)

www.mimi-gonzalez.com
Life Coaching by Mimi (Ruth's sister)

www.thebonfireministries.com
Women's Ministry by Bonnie Joy Kelley

www.facebook.com/melisa.mccann.music
Ruth's daughter's band

https://www.facebook.com/groups/JoyceMeyerBibleStudy/
Ruth's group on Facebook.

www.GraceSarasota.com (Ruth's church)
"Grace Community Church" Sarasota, Florida

www.gods-word-works.com
Ruth's official book website

Special Request

Thank You For Reading My Book!

I really appreciate all of your feedback,
and would love hearing what you have to say.

Please leave me an honest review on Amazon letting me know what you thought of the book, the index, and the free "Action Guide" (available at: www.Gods-Word-Works.com).

Thanks So Much, and Abundant Blessings!

Ruth Gonzalez-Brewer

About the Author

Ruth Gonzalez-Brewer

Ruth was born in San Juan, Puerto Rico and raised a daughter of a pastor. She has been passionate about learning, teaching, and encouraging others with God's Word for over 40 years, and has taught Bible studies since she was 18. She's an Advanced Class Graduate of The Way Biblical Research and Teaching Center; a "Discover Your God-Given Gifts" Certified Teacher; a former bilingual columnist for "El Faro" in the *Lighthouse Christian Newspaper*. She has also participated in missionary work, women's, children's, and music church ministries, and many Christian conferences.

After 2012 when she underwent major brain tumor surgery, God inspired her to start leading a Bible study at her home because of her love for God's Word and the teaching ministry of Joyce Meyer. She then started a "Joyce Meyer Bible Study" Facebook page, which now has over 13,000 followers from around the world, teaches monthly Bible Studies on Facebook Live and leads a connect group at Grace Community Church. At the same time, Ruth has also been involved in leading a Spanish Bible Study called "Nueva Vida" ("New Life"). Her goal is to continue spreading the Good News of God's Word that saves and transforms lives!

Ruth has a Bachelor's and Master's in Education from Indiana University. She taught elementary school for 20 years and was recognized in the "Who's Who Among America's Teachers" 2000 Edition; was a former "Indiana Civil Rights Commissioner" appointed by Indiana Governor Bayn in 1989; a cable TV host of the "Ruth Benavente Show"; president of the "Hispanic Women's Forum of NW Indiana"; awarded the "Volunteer of the Year" Award by the US Hispanic Leadership Institute; founder of "Retos" a Spanish class at the "Women's Resource Center of Sarasota County"; and was an Adjunct Professor at Keiser University. She is currently a Licensed Florida Notary Public, and loves helping others as a HUD Certified Housing Counselor.

Ruth is a proud mother of five children, and three grandchildren. She enjoys gardening, traveling, and empowering others with God's Word. She resides with her loving and supportive husband Dale in Sarasota, Florida.

Made in the USA
Columbia, SC
05 August 2021